A FIERCE GREEN PLACE

T0326743

A Fierce Green Place

New and Selected Poems

Pamela Mordecai

Edited by Carol Bailey *and* Stephanie McKenzie

With an afterword by Tanya Shirley

A New Directions Paperbook Original

Some of the poems in this volume appear with the kind permission of Sandberry Press (*Journey Poem*, *The True Blue of Islands*); Goose Lane Editions (*Certifiable*); Tsar Publications (*Subversive Sonnets*); and Mawenzi House (*de book of Mary: a performance poem* and *de book of Joseph: a performance poem*).

Thanks to the editors of the following publications in which some of these poems have appeared: *Caribbean Quarterly, The Georgia Review, Harper's, Journal of West Indian Literature, The New Quarterly, The New York Review of Books, Pathways, Savacou, For the Children of Gaza* (The Onslaught Press, 2014), *Gush: Menstruation Manifestations for Our Times* (Frontenac House, 2018), *100+ Voices for Miss Lou: Poetry, Tributes, Interviews, Essays* (University of the West Indies Press, 2021), and *To Kingdom Come: Voices Against Political Violence* (The Onslaught Press, 2016).

Note on the text: Except for "Walker" (published in *Journey Poem* and revised for *Certifiable*) and "Dust" (a revised version of which appears in *Poetry International*, vol. 7/8), the poems in this selection are the latest versions and not the original iterations. Certain poems, as well as Jamaican Creole spellings (which have been modified for consistency throughout this selection), have been updated and so differ slightly from the previously published versions. All capitalizations and lower case titles and words throughout are deliberate.

Manufactured in the United States of America
First published as a New Directions Paperbook (NDP1531) in 2022
Design by Marian Bantjes

Library of Congress Cataloging-in-Publication Data
Names: Mordecai, Pamela, author. | Bailey, Carol (Associate professor of English), editor. | McKenzie, Stephanie, editor. | Shirley, Tanya, writer of afterword.
Title: A fierce green place : new and selected poems / Pamela Mordecai ; edited by Stephanie McKenzie and Carol Bailey ; with an afterword by Tanya Shirley.
Description: First edition. | New York : New Directions Publishing, 2022. | Series: New Directions paperbook | A New Directions paperbook original.
Identifiers: LCCN 2022003270 | ISBN 9780811231046 (paperback) | ISBN 9780811231053 (ebook)
Subjects: LCGFT: Poetry.
Classification: LCC PR9199.3.M6358 F54 2022 | DDC 811/.54--dc23/eng/20220126
LC record available at https://lccn.loc.gov/2022003270

10 9 8 7 6 5 4 3 2 1

New Directions Books are published for James Laughlin
by New Directions Publishing Corporation
80 Eighth Avenue, New York 10011
ndbooks.com

For Martin,
David, Daniel,
Rachel *and* Michael
and Zoey

Contents

from **de book of Joseph: a performance poem (2022)**

New Poems

Early Poems

Red, Red Wine

I'd made it: it was deepest burgundy
inside my belly—six months high.
"Habla usted español?" she said
so recent from my husband's bed
young sleek untried I heard
and wished her dumb.
And in the end it died.

Now I remember mirrors, smoke,
dark wood, a crude joke
from a stool, the brown curve
of my shoulder still enough
to twist a tough man's will
and more than all my making
that fine woman child
that lit my womb, and gently
from the jukebox, "Red, red wine."

A Birthday Wish

for Colly

That the days
are bubbles
now

      not links
      locked
      to
      each
      other's
      ends
      barren
      proximities
      of
      front
      to
      back

but bubbles
each
translucent
pear
blown from
your
straw
pipe
bright
intact
passing
so slow
so quick
across
the air
pierced

on
the dagger
of
a blade
of grass.

Butterfly

Suddenly a small yellow butterfly
enters the landscape. It is redefined:
the colours are pronounced
for the first time
with absolute care,
not for science, the spectrum,
but for the original power
of making and shaping.

So grass is the green of gold
and the sky also that blue:
the purple bougainvillea
that overcomes the emerald
of this tree is orange light
and the very round
indescribable orb of the sun
celebrates what is left
when green and red are taken.

Eddy

with indebtedness to Edward Kamau
and to Derek's "The Glory Trumpeter"

Eddy
eddy
eddy plays on
a life
with his ripples
of words

catch the song
catch the song

how I listen
and long
for its rope
in the neck
of my mind

how I listen
and long
for the point
of its hook
in my throat

on some note
on some tremulous
note still
on air
still on air

blow my mind
blow my mind

with the thrum
of a drum
with the blues
black good news
of a whole
soul for me

eddy
eddy
eddy play
on my life
with your ripples
of words

watch my throat
watch my throat

Let the whirl
of your stream
catch my song

and I choke
on the note.

from **Journey Poem (1989)**

Walker

My mother
was a walker
clothes in a brown
paper bag headed
for where under
some car some
bus some
precipice
her whimsy
claimed
a place.

It ran
in the family:
her father
walked one morning—
just so—down
into the sea
left Grandma
with eleven crosses:
small wonder
(my man says)
he did it;
poor Grandpa
cut his losses.

Family Story

My father fair
with his straight nose and hair
kept chickens and a goat:
no country bakra
citywise farming for him
a sheer subsistence
enterprise

He built boats too
and houses, furniture
with those fair hands
and tended cuts
and bruises
carefully

never kiss ass
never owe money
never cuss
never give less
than a day's work
for a day's pay

all of his life

minded his coolie wife
in love to sanity.

Careful then
how you cross me.

Island Woman

I am a woman
of a fierce green place

my brows are mountains

tendrils of winding rivers
coil through my hair
short muddy black
with rapids and meanders

you may drink at the
springs of my eyes

I sing many songs
I am silent only
when the winds turn
upon me

sometimes for fear
I shiver

winds rumble in my belly
blow hot blow cool

paths vein my hands
well trod

Each year after the rains
I blossom

Kingdoms grow in my dark womb.

Chinese Gardens—UWI

Eden each morning as this place
wakes to praise cobwebs crocheted
into the grass all foliage
wet with the beads of birth

I come feet naked to the sun
my children's footsteps splashing green
seduce my loins sweeter than lust
another life another life

The condom garlands on the ground
proclaim the irony at me
but they are dead—this garden's calm
chinoiserie contains no passions

And I smile back for the tight buds
the lizard's egg bird's nest
the glow behind the hill
are things about to be

It's time this garden bred something
beyond the tremors of
an undergraduate lust, well time
we planted something here

deep as a tomb, some seed intent
on growing. I call my children to my
knees and bless their new lives one
by one. A small breeze carries
summonses. We come.

Poem

for Edward Kamau Brathwaite

It grows inside you
like a child
its meanings secret
like the peal of bells
heard
and their music
long after

The rubric scratches
on the retina
the drums sound
but no spirit starts

Until
the fingers of the blood
assort the images
the wind remembers
sifting the long grass
the womb impulses
summoning
the beast

In
a new testament
the Word

Protest Poem

An ache is in a man. Towns do not ache,
nor ghettoes fester; the ravening gnaws
at bellies one-one; hurt is personal.
On the corner again and again see me
sit with my needle and spoon, see me
puffin my spliff, see me splittin my mind,
see me teenager dead from the blows
of your words that baptize me according to
Lenin and Marx: "You are no one, no one."

Blessed be the proletariat whom
                we must mobilize
                we must motivate
                we must liberate
                we must educate
                to a new political awareness

Is de ole chattel ting again, de same
slavery bizniz, but dis time de boss
look more like we and him does be smarter.
Not a damn soul going mobilize my ass
to rass. Dem joking. Any fool can read
Das Kapital. What is dat to de poor?

We the people propose
the abolition of you
and us: we propose
an acknowledgement
of our persons and
an alliance of poverty
we propose to share the little
that breeds on these
antilles one mango
to one mouth:
we propose to speak

your language
but not abandon ours:
we insist that you
understand
that you do not
understand us.
You may begin
by not shouting—
we are tired of noise.

On the corner again and again see me stand
with my pride and my children, my quiverful, lot,
my portion of life. See me labour and wait; see me plan
and scratch dust for a yamroot, a corn, bellyful.

See me—
Look!
I am
here
I am
here
I am
here.

Last Lines

This is the last line I draw.
Alright. Draw the last line.
But I tell you, yonder
is a next. No line ever last,
no death not forever.
You see this place? You see it?
All of it? Watch it good.
Not a jot nor a tittle
going lost. Every old
twist-up man you see,
every hang-breast woman,
every bang-belly pikni
every young warrior
who head wrench
with weed, white powder,
black powder, or indeed
the very vile persuasion
of the devil—for him not
bedridden you know—
every small-gyal-turn-woman
that you crucify on the
cross of your sex
before her little naseberry
start sweeten,
I swear to you,
every last one shall live.
Draw therefore, O governor,
prime minister, parson,
teacher, shopkeeper,
politician, lecturer,
resonant revolutionaries,
draw carefully
that last fine line
of your responsibility.

from **de Man: a performance poem (1995)**

STATION I: *Jesus Is Condemned to Death*

NAOMI (*Servant to Pontius Pilate's wife*)

> Unu see mi dyin trial!
> Dem people yah nuh easy.
> A kill dem a go kill de man.
> How yuh mean "Which man?"
> Nuh de man Jesus. Yuh know—
> de one dat preach? And
> tell story? Yuh never hear
> him yet? Bwoy, me nuh
> understand unu young
> people. If unu did stay at
> unu yard, me would seh
> come. But unu walk street
> and ignorant same way.
> Me studying dis man from
> him come down a Jordan side
> and mek de Baptist dip him.
> Is dat baptism yuh must
> hear about! Dat's how
> me know is not a ting but
> politricks—dat and red eye.
> All dem old hypocrite—
> seh dem is priest and nuh
> have time fi people.
> A good ting rain nuh fall
> fi joke round dese parts else
> dem would a sure fi drown.
> So dem ugly, a so de man
> good-looking. Dem have big
> word fi throw but him
> could talk. De truth is not
> a one o' dem could draw
> a crowd like him. And when
> him ready him just tek

time and do a likl healing.
Who lame cyan walk. Who dumb
cyan talk. Dem seh him all
raise dead! Beelzebub
or no Beelzebub—
de man have power yuh hear.
Dem old and ugly, full
up of dem self; have nuff book
learning and cyaan talk three
word straight. And if dem life
did turn pon it dem wouldn't
have de power fi mek
a dead fish twitch.
Dat is de whole ting—
cash bill and receipt.
So dem send some old
criminal fi drape him up
and drag him here. Real
ragamuffin—if yuh
ever see dem! Beg yuh just
pass mi head-wrap—do. Time
going. Me betta go dere quick.
God know which dutty business
dem a knock dem wicked head
togadda fi perpetrate . . .
Is must be why my mistress send
me to report on what dem
doing to him. Me sure she not
going stand fi it. Me hear
her tell de Pilate one
"You let him die and you
will have no peace." She seh
she dream some awful tings
and yuh know dat is one
could dream . . .

        Still
pray Jah dat my future
never rest with that frog-
face for him have neither
character nor courage
nor de commonsense
fi do what him wife seh.

STATION II: *Jesus Takes Up His Cross*

NAOMI   Now crowd is not sinting
me like. No sah. First ting
dem smell so bad. Next ting
dem carry on worser dan
dem stink. Yuh woulda tink
when three four smadi come
togadda dem would encourage
dem one anodda fi behave
likl better. Each one
teach one. Nuh so? Yuh see
all me? Yuh tink is one
time me call out since me
come down yah tell dem seh
"Take time nuh man? Don't
Israelite a God pikni?
So how come unu calling
out fi blood like savage?
Brawling over who capture
who place like is Leaven
Supper unu all come to . . . ?"
Mark yuh it never mek
one scrap o' difference.
Me coulda save mi breath.
Well anyhow is Madam send me
here fi find out just exactly
what dem doing to de man—
but me will never see
not one ting in dis crush.
Well seeyah! Look who mi
eye bless! Hi! Samuel! Is what
a old smadi like yuh
doing in dis palampam?
Yuh nuh fraid yuh heart tek yuh?
Is what yuh pointing trying
fi seh?

(*Samuel gestures from afar to Naomi. She eventually understands his intention.*)

Ah-oh! Yuh know
de way dem going to walk him?
All right. All right. Me a
go follow yuh go up
de Skull Hill road so we
cyan see him as him come.
(*Arrives at where Samuel stands.*)
So Samuel is who tell yuh
is dis way dat dem
bringing him?

SAMUEL (*A disabled carpenter*)
Howdy Naomi!
Dis long long time me don't
put mi two eye pon yuh—

NAOMI   Samuel yuh sure dat is
dis way? How me nuh see
him yet? Is who tell yuh?

SAMUEL   (*Aside.*) Me see today yuh nuh
have howdy giving way . . .
It grieve me deeply but
to tell de truth is mi
big nephew.

NAOMI   Yuh sister big son? Hmn-hmm.
Me know. De one dat sell out
to de Roman dem—a do
dem dutty work. No mind.
No mind. Shaddai will mek

him see de light one day.
(*She sees Jesus as the*
procession rounds a corner.)
Jah help us! Samuel!
Look pon de sergeant
major macca weh dem
shove in de man head!
One just miss him left eye.
But what a wutless wicked
pack!

SAMUEL   Well yuh know what dem seh
him seh . . .

NΛOMI   Yuh mean him seh
him is God Son? And him
wi build de temple back
in three day if dem mash
it down? Look yah massa
sun hot round dese here parts
yuh know. Dat heat could fly
in a man head and turn
him crazy. So him get
a likl mix up. Dat is not
no crime. And furthermore
dis not no ordinary
crucify. Look how de
man back bloody up!
A scourge dem scourge him.
Samuel me hope yuh nephew
never had no hand in dis.
Ah doesn't like de looks
of it. Dat cross is t'ree
time bigga dan de

normal size. Him nah go
mek it halfway up to
dat Skull place. And not a
sandal pon him foot.
                    Well
my great-granny seh who
born fi heng cyaan drown so
dis one must be born to
crucify. One ting me know—
yuh see Talitha? Jairus
likl girl? My sister work
into dat house. She seh
de chile was dead dead dead.
And last week, a nuh she
Jairus betroth to Levi son?

STATION IV: *Jesus Meets His Mother*

SAMUEL   (*To himself as he struggles
to get closer to Jesus.*)
Naomi? Well ... How she
could know? She did mek up
her mind and gwaan her way
time me reach Nazareth.
And it nuh mek no sense
me try fi tell her now.
She wouldn't keep quiet to hear
me anyhow.
           When dis child
Jesus was a likl bwoy
me was apprentice to him pa.
A real funny 'prentice!
Me was a big man, forty plus,
wid one hand twist, de next
one chop off at de wrist.
But dat man Joseph teach
me how to use hammer
and saw and chisel wid
mi twist hand and mi stump.
... Still is de lady Mary
dat me couldn't take
mi two eye from. And so
me watch her, so she watch
dat child. And all de while
she going on doing what she
have to do. Me cyaan ex-
plain to yuh. Is like she
know dis child is de most
precious thing and like—just
how him running up and
down chasing him ball—she
seeing him dying right dere
as she look.

So me just
have to do a likl
jostling here today. Me
know just now she seeing
before her eye what she
was looking at for all
dem years. See. Is de self-
same countenance she gazing
on him wid. And him . . .
Oh Jesus, don't look pon
her so. She know yuh love
her right down to yuh toe.
She know yuh never want
to leave her so. She know
Jah seh is so it haffe
go. From yuh was likl
Jesus did she know.

STATION VI: *Veronica Wipes the Face of Jesus*

NAOMI   So Samuel how yuh pikni dem?

SAMUEL   Is ongl one godson
         me have. Him married and
         have five pikni—one girl,
         four bwoy. Handsome yuh see—
         just like dem granpappy.
         And tank God all of dem
         to de last likl one hearty.

NAOMI   So how about yuh wife?

SAMUEL   Mi wife Naomi? Wife?
         Me never have no wife . . .
         (*Breaks off, turning his
         attention to Jesus again.*)
         Well woman brave fi true.
         Dis one she just arrive
         inna de midst o' dem.
         Shub past foot soldier,
         captain and centurion fi
         plant herself braps right in front.
         She not no riff raff neither
         for she nuh pay no mind
         to all de facetiness de likl
         jump-up soldier dem a
         fling pon her.
                      She pretty too
         nuh mind how her eye red
         with crying. Come to tink
         bout it pretty not de
         word. Is a strong face.
         A honest decent face
         and dem two eye hold on to Jesus.

Well no procession going
nowhere like how she
set pon hinder progress.

NAOMI   Look Samuel! She have
one big white handkerchief.
Hmn-hmm. De finest linen dat.
Look like a foreign thing.
Egyptian, if yuh ask me,
or from de East. Is camel
goods at any rate. Well dear—
not any little cheapness
from round here. Is wipe
she take it wipe him face—
so much fi white and clean!

SAMUEL   But seeyah now! God help us.
Jahweh spare some mercy for
us wretches, men of likl worth—
look de man face, de clean
dead stamp. Look how it print
out pon de piece of cloth!

STATION IX: *Jesus Falls the Third Time*

NAOMI   Samuel mi knee dem weak
         and me not carrying
         no cross. Mi head feel like
         a hammer beating beating
         into it and me nuh
         have no macca jooking
         down into mi eye. Why
         dem don't leave de man alone?
         Why dem cyaan satisfy?
         Him shoulder nearly touching
         pon de ground. De Cyrene
         man ... Him have to walk
         and stoop for oddawise
         de cross capsize. Look! What
         me tell yuh? Same ting me
         just seh. Him flat down pon
         him face. Him *must* be dead now—
         and still de Roman dem
         cyaan leave de man alone.
         Why dem don't push and shub
         and whip de odda two?
         Two common criminal—
         big strapping brute dem.
         De likl twig dem carrying
         will never hold dem weight.
         No badda get up, Jesus.
         Better yuh dead right dere.
         Better yuh spare yuh madda
         and yuhself dat bitter shame.
         Dem seh yuh come from David
         line. Tink of yuh fambili.
         Tink of yuh madda. Tink
         of yuh good name.

SAMUEL	Naomi careful how yuh giving out advice like dat. Nuh yuh same one just seh yuh was big woman—big enough fi know yuh owna mind?
NAOMI	Yuh is a hard man, Samuel.
SAMUEL	Ah well my lady . . . As mi pa would seh, dere's hard and den dere's hard.
NAOMI	Alright Samuel. Suppose me tell yuh seh me never married neither? And not fi want of opportunity!
SAMUEL	Dat is a pity Naomi. A woman in dese places need husband and pikni. And yuh would mek a man happy. Don't yuh tink me should know?

STATION XI: *Jesus Is Nailed to the Cross*

NAOMI   Well in a way it had
to come to dis. Is so
life stay. If him was just
anodda likl madman
passing through, dem wouldn'
haffe kill him. Him mussi
really God fi true, else
him would dead t'ree time
a'ready. And now dem
going to lick some royal
nail into him wrist
and kill him one more time
before him dead. Look
Samuel. De man whole
body jump each time dem
bring de hammer down. Blood
running from him two hand
like two river. Is lift
dem lifting up de cross
now—Samuel, dem nail
so big him weight going tear
him off it when dem drop
de cross inna de hole.

SAMUEL   Naomi yuh know is
now I see de ting. Dis
crucifixion is a
sacrifice. Dis Golgotha,
Hill of de Skull, come like
de altar for de sacrifice.
And de man Jesus is de
offering. And if him
is God son fi true den
anyhow dem kill him, some

dread dread tings going come
upon dis land. So me
nah leave yah till him dead,
no matta how it bruk
up mi old body and
tear mi soul apart. Mi
time well short. Today me
must find out which priest is
really priest. Me haffe know
who have de truth, who have
de power, who me must
follow—de Pharisee dem
or de Nazarene.

STATION XIV: *Jesus Is Laid in the Tomb*

NAOMI   Me never see a ting
like dis from de first day
me born. Pinch me Samuel.
Me don't know if me sick
or well. Alive or dead.
Me tink de sun must be
fly up in my head too.
First de man die and it
get dark and mi head grow
big big. Me feel like
every duppy lef dem grave
and flying past. And den
dem take him down and give
him to him madda—and de air
on fire like it full wid
heavenly bodies cherubim
and seraphim. Samuel me tink
mi pressure taking me . . .

SAMUEL   Den me nuh must have pressure too
for everything yuh see, me see.

NAOMI   But wait Samuel. Me know
dat man. De old man wid
de long long hair—except
him head top bald. Him name
Joseph. Have money too.
Me have a friend and fi her
aunty sister-in-law work in
him house. Yuh want to see
de nice nice tings what dat
man give her. Foreign goods!
Yuh see de white cloth dem
a wrap him in? A bakra

sinting dat. Anyhow yuh see
dat old man from Arimathea
bring it come . . .

SAMUEL   Trust yuh fi know
              where de man come from!
              But Naomi if yuh talk
              so much, tings pass yuh by
              and when yuh give yuh missis
              de report she not going
              satisfy. Yuh fi use up
              yuh eye and give yuh jaw
              a break. De old man talking
              to de soldier dem.
              De man dem wid him lifting
              up de body. Look. No mind
              dem walking brisk and carrying it,
              him madda walking wid dem
              strong same way and nah let
              Jesus go. And all her
              woman friend dem 'longside
              her to de last. Respect,
              mi ladies. Nuff respect.
              Me feel it for dat lady Mary
              and before night fall
              me going to tell her so.

NAOMI   Is mad yuh mad Samuel?
              Me nuh tell yuh a'ready
              seh respectable smadi
              know how fi keep dem place?
              All me, me just going follow
              dem and look. No harm in
              dat. Dem not going mind.

SAMUEL   Well yuh was always one
              mek argument fi suit
              yuhself. Dem stop. Ah yes.
              I know dis place. A up-scale
              burial ground. Dem seh de rock
              is marble. Nuff silver drop
              fi buy dat plot. De old
              man Joseph must be love
              my lady son fi true. Him nah
              go get a next grave plot
              in dis-yah place no matter
              how him rich.

NAOMI   Dem gone inside.
              Look how de place gone dark
              again. Yuh notice Samuel?
              Or is mi pressure take
              me a next time?

SAMUEL   It dark out here fi true
              But look inside—look like
              a blazing fire in de tomb!
              Me going down so, yuh hear.
              Me going fi take him madda
              hand into fi mi two and tell
              her seh me grieve wid her.
              Dat stone so big dem sure
              fi need anodda hand
              fi help fi close up de
              grave mout.

NAOMI   Well fi mi madda bring
              me up fi know mi place.
              And is mi yard me going now.
              Anyhow . . . yuh tell him madda

from me dat her pikni
was a special child
fi true. Me nuh know if
him was God son, Messiah
De Anointed One, but me
know man fi wat dem is
and me watch nuff nuff
pikni grow. So me should know.
Dat Jesus not no ordinary man.

SAMUEL   Peace, Naomi, peace. Dat's what
de man did always say.
Yuh know, him madda
tell me when him born
de angel dem did full
de sky wid singing:
"Peace on earth. Peace to de
people of good mind—
de ones dat bless
instead of cuss." Is sake
of dat dem murder him.
Him never care bout who yuh
was, just what was in yuh heart.
So, Naomi, de whole o' we
best learn to study peace.
Yuh, me, de Roman dem
de Pharisee, stranger,
familiar, fambili.
De whole o' we. So peace
mi sister. Peace and love.
Me gone. Walk good.
Me see yuh soon.

NAOMI   Amen, Samuel. Amen.

from **Certifiable (2001)**

Tell Me

So tell me what
you have to give:

I have strong limbs
to haul in castaways
stomach to swallow time
digest the days
salt skin to sail on smooth
like morning sea and tangy
lips for kissing.

I'm well fixed
for all love's traffic.

And further, I've an ear
open around the clock
you know, like those phone
numbers that you call
at any time. And such soft eyes
that smile and ferret out
the truth. Extraordinary eyes
and gentle—you can see yourself.

It's strong and warm and dark,
this womb I've got, and
fertile: you can be a child
and play in there, and if
you fall and hurt yourself
it's easy to be mended.

I know it sounds a little much
but that's the way it seems to me.

So tell me, brother,
what have you to give?

Poems Grow

on window ledges or especial corners
of slightly dirty kitchens where rats hide

or offices where men above the street
desert their cyphers of the market place

to track the clouds for rain or ride the wind
guileless as gulls oblivious of the girl

upon the desk who proffers wilting breasts
for a fast lunch.   Ah which of us wants

anything but love? And first upon the hill-
side where bare feet in a goat's wake

avoiding small brown pebbles
know earth as it was made

and women working fields
releasing cotton from the mother tree

milking teats heavy with white
wholesomeness or riding wave

on wave of green cane till
the swell abates and the warm

winds find only calm brown surfaces
thick with the juicy flotsam of the storm

make poems

and men who speak the drum bembe
dundun conga dudups cutter

or blow the brass or play the rumba box
or lick croix-croix marimba or tack-tack

and women who record all this
to make the tribe for start in blood

send it to school to factory to sea
to office university   to death

make poems

and we who write them down
make pictures intermittently

(sweet silhouettes fine profiles
a marked face) but the bright light

that makes these darknesses
moves always always beyond mastery

Griot older than time on Zion Hill
weaving a song into eternity.

Shooting the Horses

for Martin Manley

At dawn he rose early again
and went after the horses.
He traps them manes glowing
ripe tangerine like Tintoretto
apocalypse horses-of-morning

snap-snap with his little
black box shoots the world
as it was the first day
green gold with strong legs
and a mane to be tossed
and the damp Mona plains
to be eaten like fire.

And what do you seek
my beloved, in the seed
of the day, when the tenderest
leaf of green light breaks
the earth of the dark?

What coin pulls you
wet from me, clutching
your little machine
obliging you capture
the crucified trees, their crosses
of shadows haunting
the rest of this Sabbath?

Is it wisdom or hope that you stalk?
Would you have me walk
with you?

Shall I sleep as you follow
the hooves of those shadows
the footprints of mountains
the musk of the mist
the tracks of the earliest earth?

I will leave you, my love.

It was Eve who first
murdered the morning.

Dust

And so to bed: on this
sweet tropic evening
sky the colour of red coat plum
what's there to do
but go to bed?

In round about two minutes'
time three million sperm let loose
going do some rockers
here—no lime that brother
a dead serious search
for a black egg
to make into
another nigger.

Now them have many versions
of who be the
downpresser but just now
I will forward as
a heavyweight
contender for that title
this here nigger
that I'm under.

The sky dims into purple ripe
star-apple then bougainvillea fading
bleached into fragile pallor
by a relentless sun.

He's gone the sun the nigger
and I have yet to learn
the lessons of a decent chastity.
Like the trees I follow seasons
fruiting, fruiting with the coming
of the rain that I am parched for.

Convent Girl

She was a convent girl, that's all.
Granted, arrayed against a wall
tummy tucked in tail under and
a saucy cigarette in hand,
the average self-respecting wand
inside the average room of men
would always stand and wave.
A minor talent, that, it gave
her little comfort once she knew

men liked her. Liked her. One or two
knew why. The common-herdy rest
made it a case of clump and curve
of winey waist and bubbly breast.

But sooth the girl had winkled out
the thing that made them tick.
She saw it wasn't any sexy trick
of lingering, no style of rock-
your-body, swing-your-tit
or heave-your-ass. What she
could screw so it would fit
a man was her mind's eye.

It was a dangerous oversight.

They said she was a boasie bitch
they said it really wasn't right
that such a slutty little tease
should soak up sun and feel cool breeze.
They catch her in the road one night
fuck out her life and fling her in a ditch.

She was a convent girl, that's all—
a little girl that five men fall
because she see over their head
beyond their footsole to their dread
of having passed and not been there.

She died for having felt their fear.

To No Music

That is my quarrel with this country.
You hear them say: "April?
April? Spring's on its way, come April."
And, poor things, believe it too.
See them outside, toes blue
in some skemps little cotton skirt
well set on making what don't go so, go so.
And think: this big April morning
it make as if to snow.
Serious!

That is something that must
make a body consider: if you can't
trust the way the world turn—
winter, spring, summer, autumn—
what you can trust?

When it reach April
and you been bussing your shirt
for eight straight month just
to keep warm, you in no mood
to wait one dege-dege day more.
Not when you poor
and cold in the subway
cold in the street
cold where you work
where you eat
where you sleep.

But you don't get a peep
of protest from these
people. "Well, it's late
this year," they say, toes blue
peeping out the open-toe shoe,

and hug the meagre little skirt
tight round them, shivering
for all they worth.

They don't agree with the coldness
and they don't disagree;
they walk to no music
and that is misery.

Jus a Likl Lovin

All up and down this
plain of Liguanea
the Mona moon heaving
up from the sea
it have some village
ram some likl girls
that not long leave behind
them hot-comb curls.
The big man village
ram-them making press
don't give the likl
gyal-pikni no rest.

The girls don't know father
nor grandpapa. Most times
them not much younger
than them ma—fifteen
is not much time. Love is
a dancehall song loud
on the radio a sharp
clap cross the jaw
if they're lucky
and stern instruction:
"Go and learn your book.
You want to look like me
before you turn twenty?"
The clap burning them skin
them hold them jaw and cry.
All them looking
is jus a likl lovin.

Now if nuns raise you
never and forever are
familiar texts. At seven

you can appoint
occasions of sin, by ten
you recognize them as men.
By twelve you have rehearsed
taxonomies of mis-
demeanour tactics
strategies man-
oeuvres terms of truce.

Still often in the end
not much of this is any use.
If man press you is either yes
you telling him, or no.
Say yes, likl from now
them say you easy.
Say no them say
that you cock-teasy.
No way to win. And
talk the truth all
a gyal-pikni want

is jus a likl lovin.

So don't she have
to give in?

Her belly getting big.
At school them all
talking behind them hand.
"Is fool she fool to 'low
any old man to fall
her so. Nobody tell her
rubber sell at shop?"

Never mind them.
The bups drop her
in him car collect
her when bell ring.
She know is not a thing
but envy why them chat
her and she know
not one of them have
any place to go
but up this street. Is only
time before them meet
them daddy with him sweet
mouth and him sin
against the sixth.

Sister okay. Betwixt her two
fat thighs there's nothing
but a sluice for making pee.
That's how church
has defined her sanctity.
That's how them preach
it out to all like me.

Or maybe she was
just a lucky chick
and found some loony
guy who gave her free
without her giving in

jus a likl lovin.

Elizabeth

And as for you
Elizabeth
so wise
of the
slow eyelids
slower eyes
even now
secrets
grow mouldy
in your
store:
your small
foot
not quite
ready
gait
travels
with more
than I
can gather
yet we two
waxed
parallel
one heart
one head
fighting
about the
line drawn
down
the middle
of the
bed.

My Sister Muse

My sister makes strange jewelled things
pieces exquisite of night and the first
light of morning selects a shoe-
black for good medicine and the heart
blood red of it chooses
small stones for the world
is made of them raids the grass
for dew with her proboscis
sucks indigo blue from the trench
of a sinkhole in Troy
on a throne of white coral nearby
a boy peels bananas
she stitches him in.
She loops round the curve of the harbour
today it is grey ah this
is the weather for fish! Bright corpses
king parrot blue chub and pink salmon
alarum the bay they are dynamite
dead.
  Astride an iguana
her hands on its fine spiny comb
she brings home their bodies
they will rest in the weave
in the sleeves of her bodice
the folds of her skirts.
My sister goes twice round the earth
she brings monsoons tornadoes
and three hurricanes the barometer
drops she hoots through the tops
of the trees she howls
in the hollows of hands
in the caves the graves
keep their dead sleep.

She weeps for the sadness of parting.

She is starting to spin.

My Sister Gloria

for M

1
So tell me girl who going to bring
you praise going raise up
any allelu for you?

2
Just like the Magic Man
whose fancy handwork
almost drowned your first

big birthday-party day:
you in pink organdy
a crown of coralita

in your hair stretching from
Mama's lap Mama furloughed
from mania by powders

for this amber afternoon
to steady you as you manoeuvre
Grandpère's ritual translation:

a fête to get the family
(for that read all of Harbour View)
acquainted with his latest gran.

I see you stretching out
for gold: a coin plucked from
this Mandrake's ear offered

between pursed thumb and index
finger then—poof, wave of wand—
obliterated. Gone. Not there.

3
Chile how I live to wish
them wands stashed firmly into
underpants! Please God the tears

you shed that time stood in
for those you should have bawled
this year your fortieth to heaven

when man home family
the whole catastrophe
collapse just so. Not you

though. That is just not you.
Instead, your eyeball dry
as January dust. No powder

helping you, you answer
musts of where to go who
to entrust with deadly

secrets ghosts of which one
did which deed to who
so long ago.

4
So, who going praise?

Me girl. I raise the toast.
I say you hail. I bow
to mischief moulting
in your eye to punning
purple in your mouth

to steering wheels spun
with panache to fuck-
yous flung at motor hogs
and pedals floored
under your feet.

To getting on
with getting on.

More time for you, say I,
more time and thanks
and tears
and toasts and
tintinnabulations.

For every bit of praise
is meet.

My Sister Red

My sister's supporting
the wall of the Jewish
Community Centre
on the south side of Bloor
at Spadina. She watches
the man cross the road
with a face like old snow.
He stares back like he's viewing
the Devil's own sibling.
She observes him disposing
of *Outreach* a poor people's
paper that retails for a dollar.
She sees he is selling
to one somebody maybe
in maybe a hundred that
passing him by. She smile
a small smile and she sigh
a small sigh, and she sips.
It is balm to her lips.

My sister is higher
than jets kites and eagles
these hell-blazing days.
Gloss that all of the ways:
unfolded she stands
above six feet tall
the length of her body
a tortured intestine
an organ that guzzles
her life an intricate
folding unfoldable fife
whimpers in trembles out
like shame-lady bush if

you take your foot touch it.
That sweet locomotion
mount a horse mount a man
bearing down for a child.

Too, my sister is wild
lit up bright with Labatt's
Red Stripe Red Deer Red Dog
any-old-craven canine
with scour-belly moonshine
for sale. Regard her outside?
Not a sign that the rot's
got her brain. She's a woman
aglow with a rain
of black hair that just
stirs in the burp of
the subway's hot air
as it spurts from a grate.
Not a wrinkle has scratched
at her cheek or her brow
not a tremor has snatched
at her hands: they grip like
crab louse.

       Uplifted, she is.
Yea, the last of her house
she is hearing the winds
swish-swish cross the plains
hundreds of acres of years.
She is seeing the mammoths
the mastodons die. She is
watching the lie of the land
as it shifts the drifts

of the dunes. Her body
a tepee the infant
asleep many moons.

Now many folk agree
is sake of types like she
and types like me hijacking
the provincial treasury—
is we make the budget
can't balance. In more
common parlance
minorities screw up
the numbers. Which is
true. The average
migrant family does be
more than two point three.
But you see the red girl? She
don't come from nowhere.
She always was here.

Still mountain still water
still spirit run deep.

The man sells an *Outreach*.
A snort says my sister's asleep.

Blessed Assurance

for Louise Bennett

Every day I take my time
to reach to this subway
and moved by the Spirit
seek some little space
corner or elevation
from which I send up
the day's offering.

Trust I trust the Lord
to lay a precious word upon
my lips and praise His Holy
Name I glad to relate to date
He do not fail me. Alleluia.
Hail the Soon-Coming King.
Amen.

Not a morsel of food
pass my lips since I wake
but man liveth not
from bread alone but by each
word that break anointed
from God mouth.

Black people not easy though—
that is God truth as well!
You would think from how white
people sauce us since we walk off
those ship we would know is
hand holding hand that see we
survive these many historical years.

I don't come here dirty nor stink.
True, I not young no more
and can tell you for sure
things is hard for old people

these days. But my mother
God bless her tell we from
we small:

"Two thing I could promise
you lot: tomorrow
and the day after. Make sure
you keep breathin—pull in
and blow out—and the prize
you go win is old age.
Is reward more than wealth
but make no mistake
is a terrible stage in your life.

"When you open you mout
you find spit shower out
stead of words, you can't hold
your pee when you sneeze,
and your knees giving out
when you climb up two stair.
Your nose don't work well
so every God-thing fair
or foul it smell the same way."
So she train we from then.
"Young is easy," she say,
"the wages of sin is old age."

So I following Ma and I
coming here clean corpse
and clothes. What I wear true
is old but it clean and it suiting
the weather. And I carry myself
as my mother prescribe from
them days, with appropriate pride.

So who you would think
cut the wickedest eye
when them passing me by?
Don't you know is my people—
my long-chupsing bounce-batty people!
Dressed for sin and destruction
devoid of instruction
hell bent on the Devil own path!

Still I stay for as long as man
woman or chile coolie chiney
black white I don't care
will linger to hear me.
If the Lord Jesus come before
I am called this is where
he sure going to find me.
I speak in the hope that even
one passing body have a mind
to consider the call to repentance
in these latter days. That even
one so-so backslider
will change him bad ways
relinquishing all deadly sin.
That one prodigal find
him way back to him Pa
who longing to let us all in.

Is the last train so I going home
ever speaking my word as I go:
"Roam ye not in unrighteousness
for the yoke is easy and
the burden light and the time
for conversion is now while
you might while the bright

of the Lord is upon us,
before the last darkening days.
Repentance, my brothers and sisters!
Repentance and prayers and praise."

Certifiable

"Grandma was certifiable,"
the infant said. "No way,"
said Grandpapa who dressed
the slice she made into
her breast two inches long
whose forehead bore a savage
bruise she dealt him with
a lignum vitae tray.

"No way. She had a couple
(three or four) shall we say
breakdowns of her nerves."

"How can you tell, Grandpa,"
he asked, "when your nerves break?"
"It's when your mother cries,"
I say, "and cries and cries.
You know the times?"
"And when you smash things on
the wall?" "That's when," I say,
"that's one stretched time."

Across the houses of my mind
doors, windows bang. Something
is hatching eggs inside
my ear. It has a point
and drills (I feel it)
on the drum. No, this
is not some mania.
These are the facts. You
won't believe that things
are eating at my nose
and at my throat as well.

I loved a man of forty-two.
I wished my nipple
in his mouth, his body
hard in my soft womb
my breath hot on his face.
He had a wife. My church
said No. I let him go.

I loved a man of fifty-two.
I dreamt he bore me
in his arms under a poui
pink with blooms
against a pale mauve sky.
He had a wife, he had
a son, and I am good,
so he is gone. I loved
a child of twenty-two.
He never grew.

The loves are dead.
Of no account. They stand
for all the things I want.
I want to dance. I
want to fly. To follow
rivers. Never die. I want to sing
the highest note so dogs
can hear. To stroke
the long length of the throat
of a giraffe. To laugh
till tears wash out
the pain. And laugh again.
To care for things, to make
them grow, to stay

awake until the glow
of morning covers everything.

Flies follow filth, repose
on rot. What is here
tucked between my ears
between my neck
and thighs, the flies
would celebrate.
I hate it, hate
its hot red monthly tears,
hate its puff-puff, its every-
second-breathing seething
so-insistent life. I know
like Grandmama the virtues
of a long stout knife.
And I am loose, uncertified.

from **The True Blue of Islands (2005)**

The Story of Nellie

1
Nellie eats sugar
like hearts beat.
Nellie can't remember
when she first began

to love sweets so.
She doesn't know
if it's before
or after the nice man

next door started
touching her breasts.
They were little things
like Nellie, little things

just springing up. You get
two spoons of condensed
milk and two of sugar
in your cup of cocoa.

Every morning
Nellie puts in
fat gobs of both
but she doesn't stir

them up. She drinks
the bitter cocoa
and then mixes the sweet
stuff in the bottom

into a thick syrup.
She samples this
like ice cream
relishing each

careful mouthful.
Good God Nellie!
How you can
eat anything

that taste so sweet?
Why don't you
ask the man
that lives next door?

2
Lee turned Nellie
on her belly,
stuck his penis
in her bum.

Swore to God
that he would kill her
if she ever
told her mum.

Lee was her mother's
favourite brother
and would visit
now and then.

Mum got mad
at Nellie's
screaming
Nellie's silly

tantrums when
she'd announce
that Lee was going
to pay a visit.

"Ma he's wicked
and I hate him."
Every time that's
what Nellie said.

"That's a cruel
thing to say, Nell.
Go upstairs
into your bed."

So they played
their little game
and Lee came
and came and came.

3
Nellie's going
to confession.
Thinks her soul
is full of sin.

How she hates
the stuffy box
musty curtain
wire netting

and the priest
who has no face
only ears for her
disgrace.

But this time
Father is gentle
tells her kindly
of God's love

tells her that
obedient children
always go
to heaven above.

Says that over
in the rectory
there is a
splendid book

full of prayers
and bible stories—
she should come
and have a look.

And he puts
his arm around her
on her way
to be his guest

and he hugs her
and massages
just one
breast.

4
Nellie's grown
and she's
ingesting
piles of pills

leans a lot
over high bridges

subway tracks
and windowsills.

One grim morning
feeling rotten
like her mouth
is stuffed with cotton

sweating liquor
from each pore
Nellie hops the lift
up to the topmost floor

climbs out on
the windy building
makes her way
over the ledge

looks out far
across the city
hangs her legs
over the edge

feels the breeze
tickle her hair
swears that mostly
folks don't care

knows her life
is not worth shit
thinks perhaps
it is her time
to mess with it.

5
Sashays back
into the building
feels a flutter
in her heart

buys some mace
and a small pistol.
Nellie's making
a new start.

Great Writers and Toads

for AM who forgives me

He is a writer a sensitive man
a thundering terrible intelligence
first from this nation
to win world recognition.
How he celebrates his people
our traditions our small quaint ways
in splendid rotundas
carved from our deprecated codes.
His tales are stormy edifices:
how the critics applaud his
hurricanes of wild wet words.

Beats his wife: we found her
little toad face busted in
wart-skinned and goggle-eyed
damp with the day's first showers
two jewels of white teeth
beside her on the grass.

"He says," gap-toothed
her words whistled her woe
"he says I haven't grown."

How I pray for the day
great writers are all dead
and women can cook
wash clean shout pin
the scribbles of their lives
resplendent drab
or not quite anything
on endless clotheslines
flapping in the sun.

Yellow Girl Blues

for Jane King

My mama she done told me
she tell me every day
no mind your skin is yellow
you're a nigger anyway.

Yellow girl blues
yellow girl blues.
I walking on the muddy road
in my sampata shoes.

So I grew up a nigger
please check on my behind,
my mouth, my nose, my curly
hair—I'm glad to know my kind.

Yellow girl blues
yellow girl blues.
I walking on the muddy road
in my sampata shoes.

And I go to America
and join in all the fights
sit in and demonstrate
and go to jail for Civil Rights.

Yellow girl blues
yellow girl blues.
I walk through so much macca
there's holes in all my shoes.

Dr King say it don't matter
he say we all is one—
the hose don't know the difference,
nor the truncheon, nor the gun.

Yellow girl blues
yellow girl blues.
I feel the firewater
as it soak in through my shoes.

Now I come north to Canada
my story it is true
they look me in my face and say
"White woman, who is you?"

Yellow girl blues
yellow girl blues.
I walking in the macca still
and my own take away my shoes.

Everybody Get Flat—A Dub

Where is the poem
that explains
what happens
to you when
they shoot your brother
and you hear
that his brains
spilled over the seat
to the back of the car
and you have to tell folks,

"No it wasn't a war.
No, he wasn't
caught in crossfire.
No it wasn't a fight.
Yes it happened at night
but no, not in town
out in the country
not a God soul around.

"No, he didn't launder money.
No he wasn't into dope.
Just a man with a plan
and a fervent hope."

What was the motive?
The police can't find
not a rhyme nor a reason
why they kill the man.
Just a random execution—

So, no, we don't have a clue
why he might have been killed.
Yes I guess you could say

God must have
willed it.

What? God willed it?

"No," the priest said.
"God don't will
no slaughtered dead.
God allow us our own way.

"So we turn into a place
with a theme song that say
'Everybody get flat—
dog coming through!'

"And dog mean gun
and is all in fun
don't mind poor
people have to run
down in the ghetto
every God-sent day
from the teeth
of the dog."
But I guess we have a way
to grit *our* teeth
and carry on through.

Till a bullet come
and you pray
it's not for you.

The True Blue of Islands

So here's my friend
writing of how poets
have named the blues
of these small islands.

I see him hold his pen
testing the tones
another poet set
to name them too.

Truth is those are
fake colours.
Counterfeit.
Watch and I'll paint
the islands' blues for you.

Just over from
the next door bar
my brother's
napping in his car
too tired to drag
himself to a safe place.

(Besides, this
is his island—
every place
is safe.)

Blue is the hue
exhausted
of his face
starting awake.

It is the black

and bruise
of the dark hand
he wipes
across his brow
to try the truth
before his eye.

Must be a lie.

It seems he's
looking at a gun.

Beyond his arm
the sea of night
is indigo. The wind
is warm. The stars
gleam cold as steel.

Smelt blue the shade
of this night's
lesser lights
smelt blue this
snarling nozzle
set to bite.

His mind is fuzzy.

Didn't he just
park his old
aquamarine
gas-guzzling car?
Say to his friend,

"You go on up.
I'm going to have

a smoke or two"?
He puffs.
Lavender clouds
halo his head.

He thinks of bed
yawning a grin.
That gun? He knows
it's too much gin.

Pushes the door
heaves out his gut
follows it with
a sandalled foot
stands up turns back
slams the door shut.

"Give me your gun."

The voice treads air.

"Don't have no gun.
And further to that, why
you need another one?"

My brother—fair
and reasonable
till the end.

"Too bad. No gun
mean man must dead."

Three swift reports.

He stumbles.

Grabs his side.
Calls out
"Help me!
I'm shot . . ."
bleeds royally
then dies.

Electric planets
punctuate
a firmament
of navy skies
spill laser
points of flame-
blue light

drill purple
worm holes
in the forehead
of the night.

While lilac drafts
of incense rise
my brother slips
his dark blue skin.

The dog-grey sea
licks at his toes
noses his corpse
looking for clues.

Like that old poet
wrestling the wind
I study shades
of island blues.

from **Subversive Sonnets (2012)**

Lace Makers

for Tony McNeill

At the Girls' School black and white nuns
with turned-out toes waddle like penguins on
flippers of buttoned grandma shoes and teach
us to make lace. Us is twelve girls, orphaned,
abandoned or wards of the court. We toss
pegs with round heads, silk cords fitted
inside a notch about each throat, coffles
to yoke brown necks in common service, ours
and theirs. Our warm wood castanets tumble
as lace bubbles like froth, spit threads knitting
to fashion webs of filigree. Gaoled in the shade
of this old lignum vitae tree, we make music,
giggling when we hear Sister Mercedes talk
Jamaican with her funny accent and twist tongue.

Reverend Mother Luke glares at us and declares:
"At seventeen Sister Mercedes waved
goodbye to mother, father, family
as she left home, another island in
a distant sea. And that was thirty years
ago. Ever since she has served young women here
like a born saint. Let me assure you none
of us assumed this call for fun." How anyone
could "mother" that woman upon whose body not
one hair is nurturing confound the likes
of me. Mercedes, now, she know we laugh
at her tie-tongue but she don't mind. She say
after she cross Atlantic and get off
the jitterbugging boat she rock and retch for days.

She never know water could be so wide;
never think she would reach the other side.
And then war come. Her people disappear.
She never hear from them again, know she

cannot go back. "Dis is my home.
De sisters, you, my friends, de people here . . ."
her arms a compass, stretch encompassing,
"all is my family. He take de blood
relations, yes. But see what bounty He
give me?" Her accent sewn into her mouth
like ours, the exact same as when she came.
She and the other two black and white birds
who teach us how to use these sticks enjoy our raw-
chaw dialect. They try it out. "Owdy! Unu earty?"

Meanwhile Mother Luke leans hard on the horn
of her red Ford—first woman in this whole
island to drive a conveyance not pulled
by four-footed creatures. Her long black skirt
slung in between her knees, beads furled into
her lap, dark glasses on her white bent nose,
she drive rough as any crufty truck man.
She deal out punishment—called "just desserts"—
in the same way. One day she and me catch
a fight over the strap she use to give us licks.
All now they tell the tale of how I wrench
it from her hand, fling it clear through
the window and proclaim, "White lady, me
not fraid of you. Is you should shame! How you

"could say you working in God's name while you
murder us with this strap?" You want see jawbone drop
that day! That time Mercedes raise her voice,
"Luke, why you beat the child? Look how long I
been telling you beating don't do no good?"
That sweet Mercedes come and find me up at my
grandmother's ground. She tell Gran, "Rosie make
lace like she learn it in the womb." When I reach here

and find the fashion district on Queen Street,
I make lace and save my money till I buy my own
boutique. Claude McKay say he remember
poinsettias in December. I recall red blooms as well:
three old nuns, faces flushed and wrinkled up as mace,
under a tree conjuring waves of foaming Maltese lace.

Cockpit Country—A Tasting Tour

Mapping the fjords between my fingers, you
make shore in the soft shallow of my palm.
You rest there, savouring the score, the notes
that gypsies say are the book for my life.
It is an easy journey, my forearm, but thirsty, you
linger to lick sweat in my elbow, then
climbing the smooth slope of my upper arm,
you gain my shoulder, pause like a small cat
curling to catch a nap. You wake, surveying the
terrain and see limber before you, mound
on mound of cockpit country, breasts, belly
and thighs, and round beyond the swell of hips
but well in reach, plump cheeks, a booty worth
the find. You go ahead, because it's what
you do, adventurer, no mind that sinkholes lurk

to trap the best spelunkers, for they say
numberless men have lost themselves inside
such secret caves, their ink black waters still
as death. You'll vanish inside neither nook
nor cave, anchored firm as you are. Where you
reside, breezes blow warm, regular, stopped
only in awe, in ecstasy, when something takes
your very breath away. And so, you have no fear,
sinuous wriggler, you journey on, careless
that after you, and jealous in your wake,
comes the diviner, lightning rod, great one
who conjures rain. But even if he's many times
your size, and dark, and thick, theatrical,
terrible, thunder-bearing, you know well

his staying power can't match yours.
He'll loom large, wind the wind up, crash about,
arrange some fireworks, blow up a storm,

send shivers down a poor girl's spine; but when
he's done, he's done, while you are in the pink,
ready like a good scout at any time
of day or night for charting landscape, yes,
but that done, after love, for life as well,
sweet worm who's lapped up tears, pulled mucus from
occluded passages, cleaned wounds, sucked breasts
to draw down milk and balled up food for tiny throats.
And with this, all along, interpreted
the songs written across this wrinkling skin
and sung them, every day, lively and long and lingering.

Counting the Ways and Marrying True Minds

How do I love thee? Let me count the Ways.
Way One is forty on his next birthday.
Way Two is pregnant with our first grandchild;
at thirty-eight she's finding her first way
to loving her own man. Way Three? Way Three,
Wash-Belly, is the last one to abide,
for when, according to my OBG,
you set them sweetly in my sweet inside,
for each Way hanging on, there was a Way
that saw the world outside and would not stay.
So Way Three, manic, mad, magnificent,
speaks the last lines in this soliloquy
of how your cells have swelled inside my cells,
of how your flesh has truly become me.

Will may be jealous for the marriage of true minds
but what's the harm in an impediment
or two? I think of Auntie Vida with her tale
about her bawdy bad-behaving friend
telling a lover who protested he
and she were incompatible, "Oh no,
my dear! You're not looking at this in the
right way at all." Shoulders thrown back to elevate
her beauties in their bloom, she set him straight,
"You have the income. I am pattable."
Mind's not the only measure, only mate,
and love obstructed may revise itself and change,
and change again, and with each alteration, grow.
Fixed marks make easy targets. So our love

has bobbed and weaved to pass the edge of doom.
No mates in heaven yet we have a pact.
You've promised you will not ignore me who
have loved you many ways. I, beyond strife,

will once and finally be still, touching
no mouse, keyboard, nor pen, nor quill,
no fork nor spade, hammer nor nail, nor broom,
vacuum, mop, nor pail, touching only
on God and his fine Son, consummate bride-
groom, and on Wisdom, she through whom I lit
on you, sweet other one in whom I found
three perfect Ways to love. So let it be.
Awash in honeyed obstacles, you'll make
a keen addition to the choir. I'll be around.

Zoey Stands Up to Schrödinger's Cat

Life is cheap and death is cheaper, where the sun only is their keeper.
—proverb

She says, "Zoey stand up!" then "Zoey tall"
and so she is upon a kitchen chair
a splendid coruscation at age two.
I'm Grandma grappling with Schrödinger's Cat.
It's hard because I'm haunted in the way
old age engages blood and bones and brain
in every little business of its life
with the bizarre idea we do not need
the gentleman, his here-now, there-now cat,
neither dark matter, chaos theory, memes,
the selfish gene, nor quantum mechanics
ever at odds with relativity, no mind
the latter is succinctly put: $E = MC^2$.
I put aside the putative feline

for my Zoey grandchild, her atoms volatile
as her impulse to take a flying leap
from off the chair. She is about to be
older, bolder, Icarus' progeny
testing out space. "Catch me, Dada!" She's here
and she's   elsewhere. But then it's no great feat
to be in two places at once, not for
inveterate immigrants who have seen
contrary things the same in history's way,
our language and our lives. We watch the Zoe
as swift, celestial and dimensionless
she takes to air, rowdy as any sprite
inebriated and astray in nutmeg groves,
and falls upon the cat. It howls like it's in heat

and I see why Schrödinger didn't choose to use
that staple of experiment, mus musculus,
the common household mouse. I jest of course.

It is a test in mind and not in fact.
If scientific curiosity coldly deprives (perhaps)
the poor cat of its life, it hardly matters since
the cat must have existences to spare
in its imagined state as well. In which
respect, cat is like us who're suckled by the sun,
of whom it's said, however life is cheap,
death is an even less costly alternative.
Therefore for all the world like the atomic cat
we're dead alive. But Zoey knows it is
as in dead centre, drop-dead fabulous.

Temitope

My daughter tells me, "Mum, I don't have much
more time, so I do not intend to read
hundreds of baby books." She's thirty-eight.
The girl child she is carrying is her first.
I tell her, "Love, it isn't very kind
of you to tell someone who's sixty-four
about not having much more time!"
But it is really fine. We say it is
longer than rope, this time, this word that has
no synonym, being itself or not
itself, being, rather, liminal, an interstice
between just then and a moment about
to be. But we who came from islands know,
crac-cric, periphrastic, is so life go.

And as for baby books, we never read
not one. We birthed you, named you, kept you clean,
fed you, sent you to school, prayed God you would
come to no harm. That cord of hours played out
by tiefing hands so long ago to snare you on your way
back home, full bucket on your head, humming
as your swift feet spat sand, slant eyes smiled at
the spinning wheel of huts ahead, ears shut
against the loud demanding threads of smoke
from their cook fires, "Sapling, how come we wait
the whole day and you don't reach home?" And then,
"How come you fade like mist and nobody see you
        again?"
How could we know a coffle choked your song
air buckled in your throat as you grew thin

down a rats' hole dug deep in watery dirt?
How could we know they flayed your bark with whips
rammed you between felled trees trussed end to end

seasoned in vomit, blood and shit? Our tears
spilled from closed eyes scoured pots of memory
as fitful slumber tossed our heads, tumbled our dreams.
We sought to conjure labyrinths crisscrossed
by footprints shouting still, "Time you reach home!"
We counted cowries hours, weeks, centuries.
We prayed, day-clean and dark, "Olorun grant
the stolen ones igba, a rope to climb
out of fate's pit to eat sweet dates again,
to see through green lashes of leaves your home of sky."
Olorun heard. The infant came on a red string. Temitope.

Trois hommes: un rêve

You had a thing with Geraldine but we two shot across
the parkway anyway (you let me borrow you)
to safety on the Hudson's bank. "Rive droite,"
you said, "safe for a convent girl lost in
New York. La Grande Pomme est une Salomé!"
you kissed my nose, "saucy putain she veils
her sagging bits in smog, working backhand
past Harlem past George Washington's
suspension bridge. Don't its smudged U look like
a hammock in the steam?" Drunk with the day,
my love-on-loan, the sun, I stride beside
this arrogant Kwéyol cock-bottom man,
smiling Anansi with a sweet invite. "Let me
tickle your belly button—from inside."

I never knew when you Edouard and Jacques
set off to free Haiti. We'd meet again
when my son reading Papa Doc called out
your names, three guys who didn't live to man-
age mortgages, see your kids grow, coach ball,
get a rum belly, dance merengue with
a graying love (so open, close, glissant, what hips,
what toes), sit outside in cafés on Old Broadway,
whistle the women with the proudest stride
in the New World, see Michaëlle Jean become
head of this northern home on native land;
fellows who didn't live to see the last
millennium, your proudly severed heads
displayed on poles by the Tonton Macoutes.

I wish for you three on that day of wrath,
that dies irae when your blood ran hot
into the dusty Haitian dirt, that day
New York, blinking its harlot's eye,

trolled yet another john, I wish hills blue
with mist, green with the vegetation strife
has slashed and burned in your republic. I wish
a knife that's whisper edged, a blade that slides
across your throats clean as the peasant cut
by guinea grass as he finds feed for goats
early before day dawns, a coup for love
past struggle, past the bright exit of blood
that cedes your freedom as you lose
your heads to that sweet dream of Haiti.

Poor Execution

They're scars carved on my soul, these friends
with heads chopped off, Richard, Julie,
Richard named like my bro not long before
shot through his gut. "So who want to go first?"
A small man with a knife extravagant
enquires. Its camber edge repeats a smile
a goodly devil's benefit. Forty years since
you'd slipped a chain around my neck. See here.
Photos. I have them still. "Surprise!" breathed from
that Buddha face, those eyes mild mouths under
the black moustaches of your brows. Mary's
medallion on a thread of gold, your gift caught at
my throat. Was Miss Lady, your housekeeper, the one
whose son would slit yours, that Madonna of New Day

bearing her jug, golden ortanique flame,
a glow extraordinaire, a spill of brilliance
sweet and sour like the pork that Jimmy Chen
and you concocted as you laughed at Dawn
and me wondering how you cooked so well,
so fast? She poured us glasses with a smile
that chaffed the long verandah at first light,
day glinting cool as a stone sharpened knife,
day gleaming bright as red beads on the grass,
a woman with the sun inside her mouth,
a woman with a son inside her skin,
a woman with your death in the slight bump
of belly underneath her apron's white,
clenched fist only just threatening.

Did they make you watch Julie's screams purple
as she blew out her life with every breath
she drew to keep it in? Or was it that
as you begged to go last, hoping to hold

her as they sliced a smile into her throat,
he strummed his pick across your sanxian neck
and crimson burbled your reply under
your chin? Soft ever, how did you deserve
this reckoning? Not that it matters since
you are all dead: Julie, Dickie, Brian, Burt,
Richard, Carlington, Faith, Hope . . . Call the roll
of thousands and there is no lesson we
can learn but that we did not do for our fellows all
we needed to. And we will keep on dying till we do.

One Time Jamboree—Darfur, Maybe?

Ku ya! No one celestial jamboree!
One place where sense and spirit can agree,
a corner whole night rattling calabash,
whirling, twirling, billowing cumuli
of skirts make to catch pikni any time
them little knee give out! But busha take
him staff, crook with a Janus head, a two-
way tongue, and slay them stroke by stroke. Is him
take bomb erase this marketplace where street
meet street, make it so poor we girls, houses
on fire, fields trod to dust, force flat down on
we back, we two legs bruk apart by dogs
with pestilential pricks that write death on
we womb as them condemn corpse after little corpse.

We carry them, no mind them bound
to dead, no mind we bound to dead. Expel
them like goat shit. Black dots with lecherous lips
that suck on empty dugs speckle this piazza where
we use one time to spread peanut, pumpkin,
pineapple, cocoa, corn. Ku bwana how
him set him sight straight past we labour pangs,
birth-water, navel-string, placenta, blood,
caul, trimmings that the old ones scrape
up deep at night and steal away to hide
underneath any stump them call a tree.
Come morning time, cock crow but green still in
these fields under tight lock and key until
rain break it free. So who going rally clouds?

Employ covert intelligence to track
the buds of sweat that bloom at day clean on
this grass? Marshal a force to dribble down
and damp the earth? Who going embed new posts

for huts? Run ploughs to ground? Shoot seeds
into the soil? Engage in combat hand-
to-hand with pests? Was a time once when pikni lap
around we ankles like warm morning waves
splashing in trash, leaves, old newspaper, as
them creep like neap tide up we foot. When we going put
we hand akimbo, sway we hip, beat exultation on
these drums again? When heels going tattoo thanks
in this soil's skin? Which priest going purge the curse
upon this place, give we back joy, restore we to we kin?

Remembering Nothing

for Kamau Brathwaite

> Minnesota: *Dakota, for water stained with sky. There is*
> *a continuing candlelight vigil for peace on a bridge across*
> *the Mississippi in Minnesota, once a week, every week.*

Let me remember nothing, not recall
this watchful bridge of fireflies that spans
a torrent with a name we schoolers spelled,
a pride of little cats unfettered from
the cages of our elementary zoo, who screeched
"M-I, crooked letter crooked letter I, crooked
letter crooked letter I, hunch back hunch
back I—that's how you spell Mi/ssi/ssi/ppi!"
The vigil fires watch one night every week,
week after week a humming loop of light,
bright chant against the Babylon of war.
Dakota people join the elements
to make a name for water stained with sky.
So Minnesota writes its liquid prayer.

Let me forget the brethren and their queens,
jacketed men and their fat bougie wives,
students war torn from skirmishes inside
the muddy trenches of the minibus,
beggars, vendors, workers in the health trade,
the tourist trade, the education trade,
the trades of politics and government,
joined with sweat-pasted fingers to declare
before the Mighty Eagle's embassy:
"You people better stop this war." These tilt
the forces: Arab men tortured in Abu Ghraib,
Sioux warriors cut off at Wounded Knee,
Darfurian women firked, numberless slaves
wave after wave corralled in this green sea.

Let me not recollect you ached to fight,
sharpies manoeuvring death contrivances
who conned the credulous with WMDs
to raise crusades against the infidel—
and there are those who don't believe in hell?
Those silver pieces changing, changing hands
for guns, grenades, tanks, rockets, missiles, bombs,
the miscellaneous tambourines of bone-rattling war.
All you with palms crossed by those pretty coins?
Beware the anthem rising in your throats.
Beware your fingers plucking at those strings.
Beware your feet tap-tapping to the notes.
What if the show you staged and took to play
abroad is revived on the Great White Way?

Bill Belfast and Lizzie Bell

in part a found poem

Efcaped on Thurfday evening, the eighteenth
instant a Negro Servant, property
of Michael Wallace the fubfcriber, here below,
his name Belfast although known commonly
as Bill. At time of the elopement he was in
the fervice of William Forfyth, Esquire,
and had attempted twice to board a ship
which lay in harbour, bound to Newfoundland,
but was thwarted. Likely he may endeavour ftill
to make efcape that way. Therefore mafters
of coafters along shore, or others bound to fea,
are hereby forewarned from taking him off
at their peril, for if found out they will
be profecuted, with the utmost vigour of the law.

I am a stout-made fellow, six feet high,
of a mild temper and good countenance,
my black skin smooth, unmarked by disease,
my mouth with full complement of sound teeth,
born in South Carolina twenty-seven years
ago, fled from enslavement there as a
ship's hand, veteran sailor until caught
again and brought to work in Halifax.
I own the clothes upon my back: an old
short coat, elbows worn out; duffil trowsers,
much worn; round hat; old black silk handkerchief.
Resident in this Province for ten years, I speak
softly and well, being the mark of one who is his own
person, for I am such, determined as I am to liberty.

The wind urges a night as slow as mud.
I wait amid barrels of salted cod
for Lizzie Bell, slave like me, let as laundress to
soldiers in barracks on Gottingen Street. 'Tis her

talent as healer, coupled with my own
as carpenter and cook has gained us berth
on the *Creole*, boat bound for London Town
at the next tide, a risk I have made worth
the captain's while, for just now Lizzie brings
our few things and a wallet with savings
put by these past ten years. It buys from him pretense
we are at liberty. Listen! I hear her steps and see
in the half-light, her form. What's this? Company?
Oh Lizzie? Lizzie! You've not betrayed me?

Spoiled our chance of freedom? A shout: "Stop her!"
chased by my own, "Run Lizzie! Quick! This way!"
"You there—seize the black wench! And you! After
that wretch! With luck he's chattel that will pay
a goodly price as well!" Lizzie is light
as mist, smart as the slice of Massa Forsyth's whip.
Our bags she's tied about her, in her hands
my purse and a rush torch she hurls at them.
But woe! She trips, slips, falls, fights to her feet,
head down, fingers fumbling, then turns and throws.
Soldiers scramble for gold amidst the cobblestones.
Aboard, she weeps. "I threw them all you'd saved!"
I pat my breast and smile. "Nigger head long!" Lizzie
    hugs me.
"Now we are good as any man!" We hurry up the sea.

Thomas Thistlewood and Tom

Shit in my mouth. He makes my woman put
her bottom in my face and push her doo-
doo in between my lips. When she stops he
says, "More! You black bitch, more! Shove it out till
it bung a clog inside his throat or I
will strip your back until it makes
a bleeding pair with his." I watch her ass:
shit flecks clung to the petals in that tight
chrysanthemum come to my mouth again.
I tell myself: "So many days I dig the soft
ground of her front, water it, plant my seed,
watch it breed in her belly. If one day
I have to eat the stinking fruit it voids to live,
see my mouth here. Come. Fill it with her excrement."

My name is Tom. It is this fiend's as well.
He is no person, nor no man, nor common visitor
from hell. When evil folded tight inside
its shell so that sky waters would not wash
it clean, and hid, and aged, fermenting, made
a beard, a mouth, and hands and feet and spleen,
the need to work woe on a human being,
it was hatching this snake. He sleeps
to dream the vilest cruelty and wakes
to undertake it. Devilry is his invention.
I cannot fight rapine and pillage, violence
past thought, hate simmered to its essence. I
can love even to eating my love's shit.
No yellowbelly demon unmans me. Watch me do it.

Great Granny Mac

Before Mister Bellmartin buy Great Gran
she work into the pikni gang on a
plantation that belong to Mr Serle,
a bakra man. That white man own her family—
mother, two brother, two sister, and she.
"He was a cruel man," my great gran say.
"He love a whip. The cat-o'-nine was like
a flask of wine to him. He could get drunk
with lashing slaves. When his arm hoist is like
you see inebriation rise inside
his veins, his muscles, brain, his whole entire flesh
on fire. He lash man, woman, pikni too.
Even his friends advise, 'Don't be a fool.
Why, man, you're spoiling your own property!

"'You paid good money for those blacks!'
He answer: 'So—I flog them as I please.'
One day Mr Serle take in sudden with
belly workings. When Doctor come he cannot find
no remedy. 'If I were you, I'd change
the cook,' he recommend. 'Some nigger trying
to poison me? I'll rid me of the lot of them.'
Bakra break up our family. Sell us
all bout. I bawling watch my brothers go
two different ways. I see one bigger sis
leave for Green Island; the next one they send
to Annotto Bay. They haul my ma over Diablo
to the far north shore. Me, smallest, stay
on a estate in town. Mr Bellmartin purchase me.

"The day I see him, little most I drop
down from the sight. Top hat and ruffles, riding crop,
barouche—this man as black as night! When he
buy me, I was seven years old. For days

I suffer fever in my head. Don't rise, don't eat,
don't sleep. Make up my mind to dead. Then Ma
come in a dream and say, 'Madeleine, best you let go
    of us.
Put us away inside.' I do as Ma say. Rise
next day. I still can hear her whispering,
'Madeleine.' At Bellmartin's I turn cunning.
More times they catching me with book, paper
and pen. I know if they find any slave
with them things was a big-time crime. But chile,
my navel string cut on deceit, dissembly, lie.

"Tricky like Brer Anansi I maintain,
lip quivering, 'I only have such things
because Miss Meggie cannot bear to play
with any foolish darky girl.' Meggie
is black as me but my excuse don't fall
askew on any ear. I go on with
my tale. 'She say that I best learn to read
and write—and cipher too. I try
my best, sir, though it's hard. I always likes
to oblige.' Dropping a curtsy, I open
my big eyes bold, make four with his. And I
make sure I learn to read like a machine.
Poor Meggie she struggle with words dark like
her own black skin. I eat those words like they is food.

"Time I become fourteen I cipher well
enough to help keep books for the estate.
'This is my smartest nigger.' So declare
Bellmartin and he rent me out to some
small-holding folks who are too poor themselves
to maintain help full time to render their
accounts. I never like it from the first.

I know one of them small-hold man was going
grab hold of me and take his dim-wit purple pen
and write his seed inside my abdomen.
And when it happen, Jesus know I curse
Bellmartin and his friend. It leave me just
one course. When I learn numbers I make sure
to study doctor too—I know plenty

"from doctresses inside slave barracks and
I con from bakra healing book. So I
know what to do to make ill well and the
reverse—to make well ill. I work my spell
and make Bellmartin sick. He lie there black
skin turning grey, hair dropping out.
No morsel pass his mouth that stay inside
his gorge. No spoon of drink slide easy down
his throat. When he get thin like gruel, his skin
like ashes, lips crack-up white like old paper, I
approach one night: 'Mr Bellmartin, sir?
Is me. Madeleine. Sir, I could boil a bush
I find, see if it help you.' A faint light
brighten his eye dishwater dull inside

"his shriveled head. 'But sir, if it fail and
you die, I need for you to write
a notice saying it was not my medicine
kill you. And sir, if you get well I need
a paper saying I, Madeleine Lazare
Mungo, am free.'" Great Granny Mac tell me
it was a black slave-owning man that set
her and her belly free after he own
her for thirteen long years. From I was small
my great gran was forever telling some
dramatic tale, and me, poor me, easy to fool,

take them as gospel truth. The rest indulge
her: "Great Granny, for sure you can spin yarns
better than Brer Anansi self." She suck her teeth, tell me:

"Don't mind the lot of them. I put you in
the will." When she was ninety-nine my great
gran died. At her graveside, wispy, spectral,
was a stranger nearly as old as Granny Mac,
and lighter skin but her dead stamp. "Please ma'am, are
    you
any relation to our dear beloved deceased?"
This from Jeffroy, Gran's eldest son, a courtly white-
haired gentleman bidding guests welcome at
the wake. A long suck-teeth just like Great Gran's.
"How any man could old like you, Jeffroy,
and stupid so? Look hard into my face.
I bear Ma's name. I am the first-born one.
That time she get way from Bellmartin's place—
is me was in her belly when she run!"

Litany on the Line

Bad news again on the long distance line:
a growth flourishing in my sister's throat.
I think if one can spill hot coffee on oneself
and sue the restaurant and win, perhaps
a legal eagle with a well-tuned bill
could whistle up a case against AT&T
and Mama Bell. Two years ago on this
same phone, Lizzie told me and Mary Joan
that they'd shot Richard dead.
Across the trans-Atlantic line I hear
the ocean sizzle where infected earth
burning with fever oozes pus along a rupture in
its crust. I see the flickering photophores
inside the eyes of deep-sea fish. I hear

the cries of jettisoned black men,
women and children, not yet slaves, just worth
less than insurers paid for cargo spoiled en route.
Slitting this Carib basin's diamond skin
they flung its glints aside and burrowed in.
A person dies. It changes everything.
They died. No alteration? Nothing changed?
Except forever afterwards ships, boats
and planes with trained, skilled crews
and honed and hardened pilots fell
into that grave triangle for the Human Trade.
And flying now above the blue Bahamas, look
and you will see, along a coral ridge of white,
dark looping t's, like long canoes, like open crypts.

O, lay the ancestors to rest inside
these cursive curls with litanies.
Anoint their necks, their ankles, wrists,
with sacred oil. Put wampum shells upon

their eyes and set bouquets of trembling
anemones between their fingers and their toes.
Sing sankeys, beat the drums to dredge
up greed, harpoon it like Leviathan
and beach it where the carrion birds will pick
its pink meat from its bones. Blessed are you
buried in this blue dirt. Blessed are you
who never reached this side. Blessed are you
who listen as the tribe burbles its grievous news
across these fibre-optic threads. Blessed are you.

Yarn Spinner

Inside she sits and spins, decanting gold
and silver from her wrists. Her fingers bleed.
Day, and then night. Myriad windows perch
above her head, brilliant birds. Through them
she cannot see the river pirouette
from a valley hung high, tumble, kneel deep
into a basin blue as chiming bells set in
obsidian rocks. Night, and then day, but she
cannot observe the stars, the sun. She scoffs air,
laps sweat off her chin. Straining to listen, finds
she cannot hear even the wind. The walls
leach marrow from her bones. The room
adjusts around her shrinking frame of mind.
She teases out a winking thread, curls it

about a spool, then wheels and comes again.
Rich filaments bite through her skin as she
construes the pile of unspun wool, rovings
of thought, symbols of winding cord, strings she
makes hum, imagine up a poem to twist
the tongue, cable to match a letter to
a sound, a drill that interweaves syntax
of word and necessary word, a song
to bring a measured metre to the hands
that drum on ancient wood. But this can't be a life.
Flapping flamboyant wings the windows preen
and squawk, a flock cruising landscapes she will
not see again. The river in the sun
spits, spurts, explodes resplendent as a veil

let fall to hide a bride. Marry she won't
locked in this tower where time goes. Her green
skin crawls, fluted as wrinkled sea. Once she
was brown and curious in the world. Now her

illumination is a crusted bulb
on a high wire. How did she come to this,
within without an inkling of out, intent
on weaving meaning as she strips it from
herself? And still she feeds the iridescent mound
so thick and plentiful it steals the light.
And are you sad alone? Not when I spin.
And are you sorry for the yarns you make?
No, for they keep the children warm. What if
you die spinning a thread? Die, yes, but never dead . . .

from **de book of Mary: a performance poem (2015)**

Opening chorus of male and female voices

(*Men in their 40s and 50s, wearing robes reminiscent of priestly garb. Women of varying ages in ordinary clothes. The narration occurs about 48 CE, 15–18 years after Jesus died in 30–33 CE and 12–14 years after the death of Christianity's first martyr, Stephen, in 34–36 CE*).

Female voices

    (*Addressing the audience*.) Listen, crowd-o-people!
      Tune in
    to dis heartbreak story! Walk a short way
    wid dis sistren. Help her bear her load!

Male voices

    A mythic tale, you hear,
    not a thing but make-up
    herstory.

Female voices

    Not a thing but de fact
    dat you all ignorant.
    Not a thing but dat none

    of you lot never carry a child.
    You all pump us up
    so casually

    and den for
    nine long month
    we must haul de belly!

Male voices

    But what dat have to do
    wid de matter at hand?
    You hail up dese folks,

say you telling story,
den you curse we and talk
about breeding pikni?

Female voices

(*Perversely off the subject*) From de day him born into a
    stinking stable,
her pikni lay him head like shahaph,
de cuckoo, in a next creature nest.

Male voices

Seem like we might as well
go wid your argument
never mind all-o-you

not sticking to de plan *you* propose!
Shahaph de cuckoo, yes!
Him and him barefoot crew was a true loony lot.

Mad master. Crack pupils.
Jesus & Company was a great comedy!
A bona fide paranoid posse.

Female voices

Paranoid how? Don't joke! Pharisee,
Sadducee, every power-dat-be
was out to fix de man—

not to mention de humble few
dat ups and follow him
from him preaching begin!

Imagine! Some fellows dat catch fish!
You all not going deny Roman officialdom
downpressing poor colonized Jewry?

Male voices

So is politics now? What a way
you jump round like a flea colony
dat have St Vitus dance!

Female voices

If de priestman dem never did bribe dat Judas,
no way Pilate send Jesus to be lynch on no cross!
If dem never cook up nuff false witness and lie

through dem teeth, dat injustice would not
come to pass. Is your lot did do it.
Him blood is on your head.

Male voices

On who head? After we wasn't dere.
We never response! Is him always mingle
wid trash and rabblement. Him should well

know dem don't have no decency!
He come from David tribe, come from good
family. He should keep wid his class.

Female voices

De difference wid Rabboni is *him*
have respect. No mind if is woman, pikni,
outcast wid leprosy, rich or poor,

crazy wid a legion of demon—
him could never care less.
Him bless up everybody same way.

Male voices

> Old people observe dat if puss
> and dog mix, is only to share flea
> and spread tick. Plus is nuff
>
> heavy matters we have to look bout.
> Best you all choose who tale you telling,
> for we don't have all day. So is she? Or is him?

Female voices

> See? What we did just say?
> De lot of you don't have no respect.
> Is who you calling *she*?
>
> De puss ma?
> Is somebody and *she*
> have a name!

Male voices

> What a yowling inside
> a yabba! Fine. She do have a name.
> Dem call her Mary.
>
> (*To audience.*) Well, bredren and sistren, seem is de
> bogus virgin we studying . . . Seen?
> (*To the women.*) So make we move de story along.
>
> When de tale nearly done
> time enough to lament
> de birth in de lowly stable, drag out
>
> de tragic crucifixion swan song.
> All who fool-fool will stay;
> all who have sense will leave.

Female voices
>And all who want to pitch pikni out
>wid bathwater is totally free
>to go dem tough head way!

(*Lights down on men and women glaring at one another.*)

Archangel Gabriel speaks to Mary

"Howdy do, holy one!" A voice sound
all around like it come from deep down
in de womb, in de tomb of a drum.

Cold sweat wash my whole body, same time
big fraid ketch me. I frighten
and shake, hold my breath as I wait

for de far-up-far-down-all-round
speaker to speak. "Child, you fill up de eye
of de great El Shaddai! Out of all

"womankind, de plain good
of you quicken him heart. It look like
you same one is to have a star part

"in a mystery play him write a script for.
So him send me across de deep black of sky,
a few billion cubits to ask you to be

"so good as to grant him urgent plea.
When him talk him voice beat
like a hummingbird wing!

"Jah-Jah know is not any small thing him require of you.
Dat is why I am asking you down
on my knees. He say make

"sure to ask so, and ask, 'If you please . . .'
So sweet lady, speaking for Elohim, Most High,
I fly over to ask dat you make a small fry,

"fingerling, a pikni dat will wring
every joy from de earth, every ache
from your heart. Your belly

"going swell wid Yeshua, Godsend
of de world. But is your choice to make,
is your amen to say.

"I am Archangel asking, no mind
dem insist I am Gabriel announcing. Dese earth
creature too love to take

"tings and twist to dem suit!
Am-Who-Am-Over-All, De Great One-
Who-Run-Tings, say is choose

"you must choose. But for sure he would glad
if you grant him behest and send
me back home wid a 'Yes.'"

Miss Ann, beside herself

Daughter, is one hefty load you lay
top of we. Me here struggling hard
to survive under it

for you know well as me
Deuteronomy state if you making baby
and you don't married yet

for playing de whore inside your
father house, you must stand in de door
of dis dwelling so every last man

in dis town can hurl rock after rock
till you drop down stone dead.
Is three night it take me

to push you from my womb
and me pray to Jah-Jah every hour,
every day, from dat first day to dis,

you would grow up safe
and stay good till you walk
from dis home to your own

married house. And me beg
Jah-Jah send a good spouse
to husband you and all your pikni.

And like spite, as we find
a righteous Israelite, you come wid
dis ridiculous, fool-fool story?

(*A loud rapping from offstage.*)

But is who at de door making up
dat big noise? See here Jah,
we don't need no more crosses today!

(*Miss Ann bustles off.*)

Mary has a baby boy

Well next thing you know,
de Roman emperor name Caesar
Augustus send out a instruction

dem must count all-o-we!
Dat time in Syria, one man name
Quirinius was governor.

Dem send orders dat every man jack
must find himself back to de town
where him born to write him name

down into a book. So Joseph
set off from Nazareth town where him live
in Galilee country and go to de city of David

what dem call Bethlehem, for is where
him family come from. Him take me
wid him, no mind me big wid baby,

for him say is him response for de two of we.
We leave Judith and Sarah
wid my ma and pa.

At de self same time when we reach
to Bethlehem, dis baby
decide him coming too.

Joseph ask for a room at de inn
but de place pack up right to de brim,
not one likl corner nor crack leave over.

Me sorry for Joseph! Him look high,
him look low till him find a stable and is dere
me born Jesus, wrap him in warm clothes,

give him a first taste of my breast,
and like how we never have no crib, settle him
in de dumb animal feeding box.

Anna's prophecy

A woman prophet dem call Anna,
a somebody well old, from de tribe
of Asher, arrive at de moment

me take Jesus back from
Simeon. She take one
look on him, lift her hand in de air,

start give thanks to Jahweh
and tell everybody about Yeshua,
meaning all Jah-Jah pikni waiting

for de salvation of Jerusalem. Eye-water
drizzle down from her chin
to de ground in a soft waterfall.

"Mother," she tell me, "look good dis day
on your child, him eye bright, him skin soft.
Put your nose in him clothes.

"Smell him clean. And remember him so
on de day him fall down
in de dirt to lift up Israel."

Jesus grows up

Not to say my heart never hurt every day,
but dat boy give me plenty joke too,
sometime make me laugh

till my side nearly buss!
Him did have one black puss.
Where Jesus find dat meagre boy cat,

heaven know! And him tief!
What a animal tief!
Dat puss follow him whiskers to people kitchen,

put him mouth in dem food.
If him hear any sound,
him grab bread, fish, fowl tight

in him teeth, execute a outlaw getaway,
settle down right here next to de porch
den eat till him stomach so full,

it drag down on de ground.
Course it never take long before folks
figure out dat is Jesus puss

taking dem things.
Miss Ruth over next door, is she first
complain to Joseph, say de boy cat

hijacking her lunch. Joseph say
if is true, him very sorry
but him ask if she quite certain.

"But of course," she answer. And she point
to de pile of fish bone on de ground
right beside where de cat sleeping,

belly full of content in de sun.
"Dem fish dere is what me did intend
to eat for my dinner." Hear Jesus pipe up:

"Miss Ruth, why you don't go back inside
make sure your fish missing for true?"
She look on my pikni, kiss her teeth,

huff and puff, but she turn and go back
in her yard. Jesus walk back of her,
take up station just inside her gate.

Likl more, we hear her give out:
"But me don't understand!
When me leave to come over your house,

"de fish what me cook and put down
in dis plate, gone way, done disappear.
Now me see dem back here.

"Is a very peculiar thing. Very strange!"
And she come back outside and admit
her eye dem did fool her.

When she gone, Jesus bend over, laugh
and laugh and couldn't stop. "Jesus," me ask him.
"Pikni, who give you joke to sweet you all dat much?"

Dis time him and de puss running round
in de yard chasing de ball of string.
Him answer, "Mums, me can't tell you dat,"

and him buss some more laugh.
But from long time me know how dat fish story go.
Him was doing dem tricks from de start!

Not a doubt dat de puss did tief
Miss Ruth food but me sure
when Jesus kotch up at her gate,

him just clap him hand and put de fish
back on her plate. Come evening, she tired
to talk bout how her dinner tasty!

Joseph say we should stop
Jesus from playing dem tricks
but me don't have de heart,

for me never forget what de old man Simeon
prophesy de day him give thanks
dat him see Jesus before him die.

Mary, as she waits for Joseph to be buried

Him was plenty year older than me
when we did get married. Him two big son
gone dem way wid dem own family

but him still have two young girl pikni
tumbling round in him house. Sarah, de likl one,
she is seven, and de big one, Judith, she is ten.

Dem did well need minding and is dat
make Joseph consider to married a next time.
All now me cry eye-water telling de story.

We make life together and raise Jesus,
Judith and Sarah for more than half of my
time on earth, thirty-five year.

Before me meet Joseph, me did spend
every day in de temple at Jerusalem,
for is dere Ma and Pa take me when

me was small, and vow me to serve Jah.
Me stay dere till me reach to fourteen.
Den de priest dem decide me must leave

Jah service, and dem tell de high priest,
Zachariah, is time me should go.
No, me say. Me not breaking my vow to Jah-Jah.

Zachariah, him never did know what to do,
so him pray and beg Jahweh to guide him.
Jahweh say call all de widowers dem in de land.

Him do what Jah instruct, plus him tell dem
make sure bring a staff when dem come.
My Joseph, may Jah welcome him to paradise,

him arrive wid de rest. When dem reach,
Zachariah take way all de staff dem and go
in de temple and pray. When him done

him come out and give back everybody dem staff.
What a palampam! Nobody can figure out
what going on. Den just so

a dove fly from out Joseph staff
and sit down on him head—
so dem know him and me

was suppose to married.
Me give thanks dat Joseph live to see
de two girl settle down

with two decent young man and set up
on dem own. Is fifteen granpikni
dat him bless before Jah call him home!

Jesus and me did know Joseph was sick bad,
so me make sure to weave him three shroud,
and Jesus build him coffin timely.

Him cry as him plane cedar plank
and shape dowel pin and glue
de wood box for him pa.

Jabez dat live next door, me did have
to ask him run go tell Jesus say him pa pass,
for Jesus working in a next yard.

Jesus anoint Joseph, wash him clean, trim him hair,
bind him in de three shroud. While me wait
for de wailing woman dem to come, me think bout

how dat child change my life, turn me into scandal,
baby-mother and wife, exile in a strange land,
wid Simeon knife de whole time digging into my heart.

Mary and some women of Jerusalem stay with Jesus

Dem did mangle my son, butcher him back
wid whip. It so bad, when dem done
you don't see skin or flesh, just a bright

red morass dat so meke-meke it paste
de purple cloth on to him. When dem tear
it off and put him clothes on again,

him tunic hide a ripe crimson sea.
Jesus, child! Just as well is Jah-Jah beg me bring
you down here. Dat alone is my sorry excuse!

When dem look on my child after all dat abuse
dem figure is no way him could heave
dat back-bruk gibbet reach top de hill.

Dem lucky. As dem shub Jesus out
on de road dem buck up a fellow from Cyrene
name Simon and dem collar him to help Jesus.

Sun well hot, not a breeze raise a breath—
only creature stirring is de army of fly
escorting my son, flying into him eye

getting drunk on him blood till dem plap
on de ground like black olive, ripe
full of juice. Is not dem alone drop.

Jesus tumble down too, never mind him have help.
Two, three time him fall down, and for each
time him fall, de soldier dem whip him

like a dumb animal. Is so him and Simon
take de hill, first one step, den a next,
not a shoes twixt him foot and de hell fire stone,

make me wonder who tief him sandal!
Dem travel, and we go long wid dem, till dem reach
a place name Golgotha, "de skull-pan of a head."

And is dere dem hammer him two hand
to de wings of de cross, set one foot
top de next, drive one spike through de two

set of bones, nail him down to de wood
like a warning. Den dem raise de tree,
drop it into de hole, and him groan

as de crash ravage flesh in him hand
and him foot. Dem hang two criminal
side of him, one to left, one to right.

Likl more me hear him telling de
soldier dem, "I-man need some water."
Is bad mind make dem bring vinegar

and give him. Him taste it but him refuse to drink.
Dis time him rib-dem bruk and dem jooking
him chest, every heave dat it heave.

And me scream to Jah-Jah for me vex to de root
of my soul. "Lord, me cannot believe dat is dis
me born your pikni for! El Shaddai,

"is how you so cruel to your own?"
When dem satisfy wid how dem plant de cross,
dem stand back and draw straw for him clothes.

Big fight nearly pop, for dat long shirt, it weave
in one piece, have no seam. Me did make it myself.
All dis time dem sit on dem rear end guarding him.

Now, tell me how a body dem maul so, den nail
on a tree could need any watchman?
One take hammer and chisel and a piece

of deal board, like him writing notice.
When him done him climb top a rockstone
dem roll near de cross, nail it up.

It say, "Yeshua, King of de Jews." And like spite
as de massive dem pass, dem insult
my pikni, bawl out "Majesty!

"Don't is you dat did say you was going
mash down de temple, build it back in three day?
Make you can't save yourself? Make you don't

"fly come down, if is really Jah-Jah son you be!"
So dem mock him, down to de chief priest and elder.
"Make him save so much people and can't

"save himself! If him is really King of Israel,
make him find him way down! Like how him
is God Son, why him Father don't rescue him now?"

Mary Magdalene addresses Mary's friend, Mariam

Me tell you, Mariam, if you live long enough
you see plenty strange things! See me stand
up here side of him ma, water jug on my arm,

bag of bread at my side, wineskin sling
round my neck, me de strumpet, me de whore,
me de one dem decide carry clap

from de camp to de whole holy town!
When she see me first time, him and me,
hand in hand, she give me a cut eye

would slice through any crocodile skin.
"Don't mind Mums," him did say. "She looking
out for me. You have to understand.

"Me is her so-so son!" When me hear dem arrest
him, me never think twice. Me grab water, grab wine-
skin, grab ointment and bread and me head

out de door. And me know dat no mind
how him mother look at me, me going wid him.
She could like it or not.

And you know, when me bounce into her
in de press, she hold on to my hand like a leech.
"Is you wash him two foot wid eye-water?

"Dry dem wid you hair?" Me nod, yes.
"Him say every tear drop help wipe fear
from him heart. De warm wrap of your hair

"moor him will like a rope lash a boat
to a post, so it ride out a storm.
Him say when him journey over miles

"and him preach, teach and heal,
and dem mock and jeer him for reward,
de oils you bring help ease him sinews

"and bones, ease de ache in him soul
and de burn on him skin. And him say
dem sin gainst you plenty more dan you sin."

And I cling on to her and she hang on to me,
and just so, don't is hand holding hand
how de lot of we drag we foot come

up dis hill? You and me and him ma,
Veronica and Ruth, and Elizabeth too,
and Martha, don't is we walk wid him

from dat rodent Judas bring de priest
and de soldier dem come
to de Garden of Gethsemane?

And except for dat John what him love
specially, look and see! Don't is just
pure woman around dis rootless tree?

Mary sees Jesus in the upper room

If Mary Magdalene never put
her two hand round my waist, hold me up,
me faint *flups* pon de floor.

Is not dat me never believe he would raise
from de dead, for in all of him life, Jesus never tell lie.
And is mostly dat why me did take it as fact

when he say he was going to come back.
Plus of course, how me was to forget
Jairus girl pikni, or Lazarus what he raise?

Furthermore is Jah-Jah wish him into my womb.
His hand was in dis right from de start
and he not one to do things half way.

Still when Jesus appear—
braps one minute not dere—
braps next minute in de midst of we,

my heart fly from my bosom and kotch
in my mouth! And him look so different
when me look on him face and him form.

First thing, him look so clean wid no spot
to remind of de blows and de bruise
and de battering dem deal out to him.

Den him open him hand
and me look in de red of de wound
(not a crust, not a scab, kosher dry)

and recall how him structure did jump
and drag down on de nails
when de cross did drop into de hole!

And me gather de jolt in my body again
for me certain is him choose de cuts
to remain as a sign

of de cost of de cross,
as a love bite bright into him skin.
And me think, *What a business, dis sin!*

True, dat signify, yes, but it was
of de least consequence,
for de rest of him look

same way as de day him did born,
like a light beaming out,
like him body could barely contain

de self of de somebody inside,
like as if already he
was in a next place,

far from here. Me recognize him
as de child of my womb while me don't
comprehend him at all. He smile and

his mouth form de word, "Mums."
Me smile back and open my arms wide
but he shake his head. No.

"Peace, bredren and sistren,"
he say. "Peace unto you." And me feel
de room fill wid de deep of de sky

on de day de archangel did fly
from eternity into my father yard
and put question to me.

———

Closing chorus of male and female voices

(*Men and women in their places as lights go up.*)

Male voices

Make we done argument,
end dis disquisition
on a make-up virgin

wid a dubious tale.
We done waste
enough time already.

Female voices

Don't know why Mary story annoy
you so much?
Is your conscience, maybe? Is because

you feel shame? But *you* never kill him.
You declare it a likl while back.
None-o-you is to blame.

Male voices

Back to Jesus again?
What rot all-o-you brain?
How much time we must say

is de mother story
we recounting today?
Is you all set de course.

Female voices

Like we say already
parenting
not someting

you have insight about.
Mary no have no story
wid her pikni leave out.

Male voices

If it wasn't for she, true, him would
never born. You know how much discord
and disruption him cause?

How much chaos him one occasion
wid him stupid good news?
A fine king of de Jews—riding one jackass!

Stumbling to dat vulgar display on de cross
at Passover! Bringing we high holy days
and we ancient tradition into disrepute!

Female voices

She did take a brave plunge.
Have pikni and him grow,
turn big man, collect up a dozen

ordinary folks and send dem out
on de road wid a message of love
and forgiveness and peace, feed a crowd

here and dere, preach a sermon or two,
do a likl healing, den die on a cross.
Whether rise or don't rise don't put food

in your gut nor roof over your head,
so it hard to know why, after dis
long time pass, you all still in a stew

about what de man say or did do
or not do. And is her story, yes,
but her son is de star.

Male voices

Every good Jew man know de Law say
take a eye for a eye and a tooth
for a tooth, fair and square.

Den dis fellow arrive telling folks
if tief take dem tings,
dem must not take revenge,

saying turn de next cheek
when a man take him hand
and box you cross you face!

Plus him run wid low-life
and make a mockery of de faith
of we fathers, dem rule and decree.

Female voices

But how dat affect you?
What it can have to do wid de price
of fresh fish in de market today?

Male voices

Don't play like you stupid.
Just like *she* proclaim she well glad
to be ma for Jah-Jah one pikni,

same time as she mourning
dat a knife cut-cutting through
her inside, won't stop—

now how dat could make sense?
Same way dis man capsize
de way we been conducting affairs

from we roam wid Moses
through de wild, and him bring
Jahweh Law write on de two tablet.

Nurture your enemy?
Forgive who do you wrong?
Dat can restore Israel?

Make we nation strong?
Who him think him is?
Moses or Elijah?

Female voices

Story have it to tell dem same two did appear
on a hill top near here and dem chat wid Jesus.
Him did shine like de sun. So dem say.

Den Jah-Jah voice proclaim, "See my son
who me love! Hear what him telling you!"
Three apostle was dere. So dem say.

Male voices

Superstition. Hearsay.
People like make up story, invent
every kind of marvel.

Female voices

Have it your way. Okay. But him stick in you craw.
You all choking on him while you hold
on to Torah, and Prophet, and Law.

If it wasn't for him, woman like all-o-you
would never lose dem pass interfere
in matters beyond what dem pea-brain

can manage. Not a thing but mayhem
and madness ensue when people
do not know dem right place.

Man is man. Man in charge.
So Jehovah ordain.
So de Torah declare.

Your Jesus dead long time.
We run things as of now.
Who have ears better hear.

Female voices

What you all going do?
Stone we down wid rockstone?
Crucify we for de whole world

to see? You think people stupid?
Dem will quick figure out dat authority—
meaning you reverend folks—

couldn't manage we poor
likl female posse! De whole town
and country and empire going hear

you can't keep good order
in your yard. *You* going see
how quick *you* lose de work.

Male voices

Exactly why dis Yeshua business
must stop. She come wid her one son
miracle baby—for she still a virgin—

wid Jah-Jah as him pa!
Him say him is a king but him have
no riches, no subject, no territory

for him "kingdom is not of dis world . . ."
paradoxically! But den dat
is him trade. Treat your enemy good.

Forgive all who wrong you.
Love your neighbour who turn
out to be every old

sore-foot man, every stink bag-lady.
De man was off him head.
Your Jesus was crazy.

Female voices

Old folks say you can lead
jackass go a water
but you cannot oblige

him to drink. At de risk
of imprudence, you lot
and jackass

have a good resemblance.
You think tings

going
roll
back?

(The women laugh and walk off singing the Jamaican folk song
"Woman a heavy load . . ." Lights fade on the men looking pompous,
indignant.)

from **de book of Joseph: a performance poem (2022)**

8

was a long time before me discover de life of de wood.

it sweet my nose right from de first.

as de shavings curl up from de plane sliding true down de grain of cedar or acacia or pine dem summon de earth and de wide open sky and de growing of green.

all de same me work wood for more dan three year before a shape sing down my arm connect wid de board make de bloom of itself.

before me hearken as wood yield and reply to de hammer de saw and de plane.

12

me was glad in my life.

den me turn seventeen. Pa say look for a wife.

Ma was sprightly and spry so me never know why him get it in him head me must get married. is not like Ma need help in de house.

true my bredren Eli dat come first did married long since gone to Hebron to join him wife family business.

de last one Jonathan did answer circumstance when him marry Suzanna one year gone. de two family-dem gree she best stay at her father yard for she was well sick wid de child and is two meyaldot her ma and grandma in dat house.

it leave me Ma and Pa but we three going on good. work eat sleep and play. pray three time a day shaharith minhah and maarib.

but me tink Pa did fraid me would fall into coarse company. Roman soldier-dem was a vile lot. some of Israel youth did take to dem ruinous ways.

"if a man satisfy at him yard" Pa was helping Ma make up a fire one night "him not likely to run down de road and look woman . . ."

Ma kiss teeth. "Jacob you and me know plenty Jew leave dem good spouse a-yard and walk street to go find a next bed . . ."

"wife is him one leave wid we and me love him bad. me must do right by him. de bwoy need to lie down and rejoice."

14

black hair wid nuff twist tell me some son of Ham interfere in de line
a long time aback. not a curl but it tease and play catch wid de light
and delight as it long down her back.

she was brown as a nut wid small breast and broad hip and puss eye.
lazy and impudent.

not pretty but velvet and sharp as new wine.

first time me see her she did look straight at me—no eye-to-de-
ground back of eyelid half-close and prim.

it don't reach my face but me feel my gut grin.

and me straightway give thanks to De-One-Dat-Run-Tings for me
know in my heart when de sistren and Ma was scouring Galilee dem
was walking wid Jah.

23

Debs belly grow a next time but de bwoy chile slip away.

me get well wrathed so me address Jah again.

"Elohim you romp rough. what me or my wife do to you? why you capture we offspring like wild dog grab gazelle?"

i double my two fist and shake dem at him.

Debs frighten for so. "Joseph you can't address Jahweh in dat reckless fashion. mind you make him worse vex!" and she beat her right fist on her breast tabering.

"after Jah-Jah is not any small time despot. King of Kings Lord of Lords have better tings to do dan to hold feeble protest gainst me and gainst you!"

25

Debs bad luck wid borning baby never change. when she lose a next one after Sarah me beg her hold up likl bit.

"hold up? but Joe is not me to hold *up*. is you or is me doing de holding down here?"

"i do not recall ever holding you down Debs. seem to me we did gree on any holding betwixt you and me."

"talk truth me love have you in my belly Joe." and she laugh like water jumping down de Sa'ar Falls.

she could be bad-behave when she choose my Debbie!

"but Joseph my spouse must i now understand you telling me you desire a next plan?"

"i am telling you Debs your body don't make from rockstone. me love loving you more dan life but me rather not kill you wid making baby."

"Joe me tell you nuff time me rather dead fat wid a baby dan live wid a man me can't sweet wid loving."

and Debs push me down flat.

29

me wait and me watch till de fire decay and my chin touch my chest.

when morning light me go down to de shop like me custom to do. at about de third hour Zeke and Aaron come to collect me behind two broad smile.

"come Pa Joe. Ma say time to break fast."

me careful to put down de chisel. go wid dem to de cistern. we all wash we hand good go inside to see Debs setting food on de table. Judith and Sarah paste to her kethōneth gazing on de new baby bright in her hand.

we sit down. me open my mouth to pray over de bread.

a voice pry my eye open. bring me into de day.

"we well sorry Maas Joe. Miss Deborah gone and she take de baby."

30

rake my heart when me tink how Debs die bringing we last pikni den like crosses de baby die too.

i send my mind back to my shepherding days.

fire water sharp knife and a clean stretch of cloth or animal skin and a pan of water. make no difference de animal kind. dem come into de world de same way.

and me have so much practice me can do it now wid a rag tie to blind my two eye.

me know me did do what de baby did need.

but if midwife was dere from de start maybe Debs and de chile wouldn't dead.

den me hear her clear-clear.

"not so Joe. was my time. was her time."

31

Debs and me share life near to seventeen year and each year it out-pass de last one. we wake work and worry. fight and make up.

make and bury baby.

it all done in de split of a meagre minute. so breeze drop and flame die so Debs flicker away.

me wail for de short perfect weave of we life.

46

de Roman-dem say de gods use we for sport.

all who know Jah-Jah know him love to play games but Elohim don't take we make joke. is true we is clay in him hand and is true him do as him please.

so tings work de best way when what please El Shaddai please you and me too.

best endeavour to do what Ten Sayings prescribe. best to praise and give thanks and surrender all tings to his mercy and gracious provision.

same so me strive to live all my life.

top de mount on dat sweet green afternoon Jehovah set him hand down upon me tired pa of two youth and two likl girl pikni.

change my life after dat to a tale mighty strange.

50

high priest wait till de widower-dem shut dem mouth.

"men of Israel behold Mary dawta of Maas Joachim and him good wife Miss Ann of de town of Sepphoris. dem did bring dem one dawta to dis holy place when she was three year old and leave her to serve Jehovah Most High.

"she serving Elohim from dat day to dis.

"but we know in Ketuvim Qohelet instruct dere is a time for everyting. a time to born and a time to die. a time to plant and a time to uproot. now is time for de dawtas of Israel dwelling in dis holy place and grown into woman to return to dem yard to married and raise up pikni.

"men of Israel when Mary hear is time to go home she say no she do not plan to stir. she insist on de promise her ma and pa make when dem vow her in service to Jah. and she further declare she her own self did promise her body and life to Jehovah.

"say no way she can don't keep her word.

"only one ting to do as high priest. i fall on my face in de Holy of Holies and beg El Shaddai for counsel.

"and behold in reply a voice sound through de Court of de Priests and de Court of Israel and de Court of Woman. it say every last widower in de land must bring dem staff to de temple and lay pon de altar. de Spirit of Wisdom will choose one wid a sign. whomsoever dat branch belong to is de spouse for Mary.

"so i send out de word to all Galilee and Judea.

"widowers of Israel forward up as Elohim instruct and rest all de staff-dem pon de altar of Jah."

59

is Mary self tell me.

she was praying one morning bout de sixth hour and a supersize angel just splash down same time bright like sun black like night. she well fraid so she put her hand over her eye but him tell her don't frighten. say him come from De-One-Dat-Run-Tings to put question to her.

see me here well confuse for dat is plenty news! but seem best to begin at de last.

"what kind of question?"

she say Jah send Angel Gabriel to ask if she will agree to have him baby.

me say "hold down Mary. tell me one more time?"

so she say de same ting a next time word by word.

"Mary is joke you running wid me?"

"Joseph me serious as any shofet sit down in a trial to judge."

76

we reach Bethlehem at bout de ninth hour. me make haste and find Jonathan inn and me knock and call out.

while we waiting i lift my wet wife down from de donkey slip her arm through my own so she can lean on me.

Mary hand on her belly. de baby low down so me know him soon ready.

we wait. when me no see nobody no hear not a soul me call out again. after one long time pass Jonathan first son Amit push de door.

me clap my hand and lean forward to greet him.

"cousin give thanks! i so glad to see you. dis is Mary my wife."

Amit eye go straight to Mary belly.

"Jah know we well tired. we done nyam but we tired. Mary have to get rest for she soon born de baby. you can see for yourself."

like how him eye don't leave Mary middle till now.

de bold face youth tell me him pa sorry but de house choke up wid fambili come for de census.

likl most me punch him!

when me look back of him me see three mean eye woman staring at Mary. if bad looks could damage dem would maim she and Jah pikni.

but dis not Galilee? susu can't reach so far bout Mary and dis pikni?

"de best we can do for de two of you is de animal shed over so."

as him point me turn tail never say no tenky. lead my wife and de donkey to a bruck down shanty up gainst de hill face.

80

Mary put Jesus on her breast.

him dere sucking lively as him two shiny eye travel over de place—a scrabble of deal board attach to each side of de cave mouth to fashion a shed.

him take in de donkey couple sheep in de corner and three brown sleeping fowl in a roost on de far side rock face.

talk truth is Jesus make me see de poultry for as him eye march me follow de journey.

and i smile and bless Jah for chicken is kashrut and if luck is wid we breakfast for my wife is one fresh boil egg.

Mary feed Jesus and him turn round feed she!

likl more and de two of dem drop fast asleep a hen wid a chick tuck under her wing.

me wonder if Mary going one day set my son to shelter same place.

106

dese last days Mary pining can't stop look for Jesus. she not saying nothing but come early morning me see her stand in de road hand shading her eye chin tilt up and gaze stretching out.

same ting when sun depart at de nine hour cool before night come down and start de new day.

"my beloved you know him don't gone forever. him will show you himself in good time. him own time."

"is not fret me fretting Joe but me miss him. my eye long for de day him fill dem again."

"him will not abandon we Mary my love. and is Adar a good time for us when him leave. me sure you will not see two more pregnant year before him come back."

"me can't wait so long Joe. de next pregnant year is two twelve-moons from now. me can't wait so long."

114

talk de truth me well glad it come like it come.

morning light. me was in de shop early for me promise to fix a table for Miss Rachel. is not any big job and me know me could finish before me and Jesus set out for Sepphoris.

me not too long working when me start draw breath hard.

but still anyway my hand firm on de saw two eye measuring de plank of acacia wood long and strong. a fragrant shalom to de morning.

next door to my bench in de grass my pasero slim papa goldfinch croon him morning song "boker tov boker tov" wid him yellow black wing and de red round him eye a headscarf of blood.

me was tinking bout Aaron and him music and Zeke in de pikni classroom. me was tinking on how Jesus travel so far to de island of Pharos wid de tower of fire and sail long on de sea to de great rich bazaar in de east.

hit my brain just like dat. fierce as fire. me did try move my mouth to call out but my mind instruction never reach to my talking string-dem.

den me look for de last.

each ting was itself. me perceive de mind and de meaning of each. every hammer and nail. anvil. awl. water jar. de blue pitcher Jesus make wid him ten teenage finger laying coil upon coil of de white yielding clay. gluepot. goo of glue. grass wid powder of wood. sky deep like a dream. like a story. de place of repose Sheol calling to me.

me member Debs de first time me did see her. spirit loud and proud and de shout of my loins when she and me join. feel de terrors.

travail. de babies dat come. de babies we give wrap up warm in we tears to de dust of Adam.

member Debs when she say she don't married to lie down wid no cat and de love we stoke dat very night. member Debs as she dying bequeathing me Judith and Sarah to raise up.

member Mary first time in de temple. her brown like a queen. her green as a meadow. her young as low tide and her old as Ketuvim preserving Solomon Song of Songs.

member how me catch Jesus sliding from Mary womb. plunge my knife in de fire and de wine. slice de cord. de knot what me tie on him belly. son of man son of Jah fill de space betwixt my small finger and thumb.

member how Jesus did love pat de lamb-dem in de market down de hill in Assiut. how me learn him and Mary de old herding tunes as stars button de sky and we rouse a new moon put a old one to sleep.

member Jesus one day de sun in de synagogue blue tzitzit on him garment as him chant Torah. Mary as tears slip down her cheek down her chin down her neck silent stream wetting up her simlāh.

den my son in a trice wid him back bloody up from de slash and de lash of cat o' nine tails as dem tear way him flesh from him bones . . .

and as quick a road wid a light at de end.

new day as sun set.

New Poems

Africa Poem

How do my poems represent the spirit of the continent? Come sound the sentences and see—they use as many languages as she does! And man has lived as long in them as the first fire-kindling humans in Wonderwerk Cave, drilling the hills of Kuruman. They feature not one single hut on any crumbling hillside but a throbbing heartful village, bound around safe in its macca-laden lesaka. No ancient city walled of stones keeps secrets better hid. In pain, rivers as wide as Isa Ber bid their eye-water up from navel springs that drizzle, shower, grow to rain, tumbling deep like Smoke that Thunders, the white queen's stolen waterfall echoing between Zimbabwe and Zambia. They are the Nile, a roving stream mile after sinuous mile turned and returned to find their destiny in a roiling rambunctious sea. Islands history set adrift, small volumes poured in air that's wet, last reaches of the planet's alphabet.

Hard Nut to Crack

Virginia McLaurin, 106, visited the White House during Black History Month, 2016, and met President Barack Obama and the first lady, Michelle Obama.

"Is baby blue, Ma! Going to suit your
dark skin to a T!"

I think not such a thing. No. Not no baby blue
nor powder blue nor blue like sky or sea. Put me
in that cloth there. Electric blue.
                                    Going take
my five score year and some, my red long nails,
my two corn pickle foot shod in tough boots
like any working mule, going go in that White
House and shake that young black fellow hand
and say, Mister, look what I live to see,
a thing I swear would not befall before I go
under the dry earth burying me right
where I born.
                    That said, I come to visit you
and your missis in fighting form. All them
who see me here shaking a leg with history
best know I come about who shoot we in
we breast, heart, head, leave we to dead,
spurt blood as they butter our life on their
new bread, share apple pie under the shade
of forest where rope wring we neck.

Jesus say don't carry no weapon, wield
no knife, court strife, neither study revenge. He
never say not to carry a testimony on my back.
This flag I wrap around my ancient flesh
is a message for murderers to break their brain
with ciphering. Some nuts is hard to crack.

Blood Claat

They swear by
woman's parts
and menstrual rags:
bumbo hole
rasshole
rass claat
pussy claat.

Perhaps like
Québecois
they swear
by what's
most holy?

Perhaps
rass claat is their hosti?
And bumbo hole
their tabernac?

Perhaps
at heart
they fear
fucking
a woman
is a sacred act?

Sword on the Road

Tommy Barnett was a 22-year-old black man
fatally shot by police on Jan. 10, 1996,
near the intersection of Bathurst Street
and St. Clair Avenue West. Police
claimed he was unsheathing a sword.

Forward yellow red and green
don the cape, make I-self seen
take a staff and strike a blow
for freedom, justice, peace and show
that Babylon can't keep I back
never mind I poor and black.

Jah see I take the road today
sword in hand against the fray
Jah see I chant down ignorance
behold I-and-I do a dance
before Selassie God Most High
Lion of Judah Ras Tafari.

Jah hear the iron stone assail
the sacred temple of the I.
Jah see the flood of Israelite blood
burst like a fireworks in the sky
scatter like sparks of crimson night.
Jah see the I explode and die.

Still forward yellow red and green
don the cape, make we-self seen
take a sword and strike a blow
for freedom, justice, peace and know
downpresser can't keep Rasta back
no mind how Rasta poor and black.

Toy Boy

Look how much time Ma tell me
is a wicked risk me run
anyhow me make the pikni
play with toy gun.

Come late All Saints' Day
Halloween parcel by post
decorate down one side
with a broad smiling ghost

a mean skull and crossbones
with a warning wide grin
on the next. "Is him father!"
me flare. "God know is no sin

"nor no lie when me say that man
never notice him son more than so.
If him send something for Marcus,
how me must tell him, 'No!

"Is your toy, yes, my love,
but you can't play with it?'"
Ma don't see, me don't see
when him take time and quit

the house and the yard.
"Marcus! Son! Time to eat!
Wash your hand and make haste!"
No sign of the boy. Ma and me scour street

school ground, church yard, graveyard,
gully-side, grieving sky.
I did know from we start. I search
with a stone heart, two dry eye.

That time him long dead on the carrion
whim of a careless woman.
"Short black man in the park
with a lethal weapon ... "

Bawl Woman Bawl: A Lament

after a Caribbean digging song

True man give thanks him able lift
hoe machete sound two syllable
as bomma raise the tune and call

say "Baby dead on the railway line!"
and chorus sound as we pickaxe strike
"Bawl woman bawl! You baby dead!"

Dry ground is drum as we pickaxe strike
sing how them bury the poor baby
and ground is drum as we slap we heel

entomb a next and a next baby.
For music wail in breeze and stream
on sand on stone on paging sea.

Ma say, "Alas for who don't sing
and die with music lock in him."
We wouldn't live but we raise a tune

to move we foot else we tumble down
fetch water scrape up wood to burn
pray the dutty to raise a crop

we walk to drink we walk to eat
go hospital to die or drop
so thank you Jesus for we feet
we moving them until time stop.

Bawl woman bawl! We pikni dead!
Pick anywhere, town or city,
dead in them high chair, in them bed,
in them backyard, at block party.

Ma say, "Alas for who don't sing
and die with music lock in him."
We can't live less we raise a tune
to move we foot and struggle through

work all night long until day clean
hotel hospital factory
scrub floor cut cane pick coffee bean
work till we drop to feed pikni.

And still no mind them hunt we down
bulldoze we choke we batter we,
empty them bullet in we back,
time and more time with impunity.

Law is for them but not for we.
Futile protest we liberty.
Bawl woman bawl for we baby.
Bawl for we know them won't come back.

Bawl woman bawl! We pikni dead!
Bawl woman bawl! We pikni dead!

Shakuntala

Maybe it come in the blood.

Poet child or Eastern labourer
in me love magic names
appellations to start spirits
abracadabras open sesames.

I know I know this Shakuntala.
But is wait I wait till
memory serve her genius up
conjurer with numbers
miracle accuracies
to the umpteenth degree.

I run here to set this down
set it down but the application
don't open and I fraid to lose
this baby for them don't hardly
catch in my belly no more.

I remember the little pikni
who run to his just-born sister:
"Tell me bout where
you come from. Tell me, quick!
Every day I forget a little more."

Learned upon Bleeding

Hot water will set blood.
Use cold. Rub
with brown soap
then flaunt on
bleaching stones:
sun-hot will whiten
everything but sin.

A tampon can get lost.
In you. Hang on to its tail-
string as dreaming
to the navel leash
on the small
almost child
for which you bled.

Women together
in one place will
bleed in solidarity
till every last body
turn super bitch at once.

Wayward is in our red;
lucky we shed
just our own blood.

Sonnet 129

Gyal too too nuff sake of dem give
her book to study fore she able
hold her head up good.

Shakespeare, she now declare, psalm
1 2 9—Lord, no, is poem, not psalm . . .
or is proverb? Anyhow de number right.

Me hear her say something about
expensive spirit and me think
she say "a waste of shame,"

say it all come with lust
in action. Well, we know that one:
know man grind woman down

leave howling presents
to the left and right and hand
middle stretch out into the centre.

Me say me not able for no
man climb into my belly give
me pikni and mash up my life.

So shame not wasting if it serve
to help me hold my course.
Plus my spirit gone past

expensive. Any man
want taste that wine pay
every last penny him have.

Not for Everybody

Look where I reach
is only some can come—
not even plenty some.
Just few. Me, you
and who we say.

Ask any market woman
how tomato stay
when every Quaco
and him cousin
touch-touch it up.

How I did fool!
One mango
to one mouth
me say one time.

How I could
think good
fruit could be
for everybody?

Come, Child

for Geoffrey Philp

Sun gone down

Land little while back
burning gold
turn green again
quiet like coffin.

A flock of ibises
blaze through
diluted blue
slow waves
not a sign
of a cloud
in the offing.

Somebody say,
"What a way
night fall soon, eh?

Come, child.
Come to your yard."

A Different Noise

We make a different noise. Is not war sink
we into this blue dirt nor recklessness nor nature in a fit.
We bury deep because we wouldn't fetch enough.

Not a place else where bones roll over bones
down in the darkest deep because up so our dried
out bodies on the block would be too spare.

Is not no susurration all the same. Like Tom King say
that inconvenient royal Injunman we are a public lot
    telling
our public tales no private story quiet on a page.

True word. From all the way down here. You think
say dead can't talk? We breathing in your kitchen
    cooling
capons fingernail's burden slid into your soup.

We're like the nasty nofaskoshun negro man
black royal loyalist whose cousin fair bloodied
her blonde hair parted with a gun.

They are indifferent to our different noise. *It was so long
ago. Your backs have healed. You've screwed our wan
wives, dinged them with your donkey dongs.*

*The world's browned up, so shit—why can't you just
get over it?* But no all time of day all up to middle night
    and day
again we here drumming rattling rattle-bones.

"A Pig a Pearl"—A Native Myth

Macko did love a good woman.
The ultimate expression
of this affection
was when a beauty
pass him in a bar,
Macko would open
his mouth wide
and call to her,
"Come, darling!
Hawk and spit inside!"

"God, Macko man!
Suppose some woman
hear you, cough up slime,
deposit in your mouth?"

Hear Macko, "You know we have
a way to say, 'Don't cast pearls
before swine'? Well every
now and then you find a pig
that love a pearl. Phlegm come
from out good mouth
don't have no price."

Legend has it he died
mouth open wide.
Pearls lined his throat.

True-True Love

after Edward Baugh's "True Love"

What kind of love that's altered by a snore?
Impeded by a belch, a stinky fart?
Passion and tenderness and more
by far impel the hand that wipes a lover's ass,
mops vomit from their lips, clears crust
from their eye corners. Love's a mess.
Spittle in kisses. Spunk the end
of every ecstasy. Each day to wake again
to find affection's proof: puddles of pee,
shit's squishy melting rocks. Get up once more.
Restore sweet airs. All other love is vain.

A Light Full Day in May, or What's True, Pussycat?

Nothing is firm. Not your life
nor the story of your days.
You thought you were his wife;
your family—you, he,
two boys, two girls.

And then one light full
day in May she
came and brought her three,
her marriage paper,
letters, photos, birthday
cards and billets-doux.

A true history.

There is no doubt
this child is his
—the flying ears—
and this one too
the light green eyes
even the little pikni
with his shapely calves
his sturdy thighs!

And seeing him inside her life.
Morning, my dear?
Morning, my love?
G'morning pussycat?
So how you do today,
my turtledove?

It could be she.
It could be me.

He let her touch
his bellybutton?
Tickle his armpit?
Pant into his ear?

It could be me.
It could be she.
Thing is we are all of us his.
We, them, she, me.
He makes us who we are.
He makes us seem to be.

Thing is for all of us the life
we had it passed away
forever after never
no sunny day in May.

Transcribing the Letters of
William Alexander Bustamante

a poem in dactyls after Marie Ponsot

Listen. I telling you. Papa and he
squeeze up like sardine in Doc's surgery
patients impatient at their company.
Chief him dictating to Papa like so:

Lulu, white people them too damn deaf-ears.
Greedy and selfish and too damn deaf-ears.
Black people starving, man. Bakra must
know dat we not gwine just lie down and
take the licks so.

And he grim up his face.

Say what you like Chief. I
am sure to get what you saying note
down on this paper. Don't fret.

Busta dictating and Papa replying just so.

That being so, Rich, how nobody know?
Nobody put it in Busta's bio?
Don't is right they should write it
if is so it did go?

Don't be a dope, sister! Nobody
sensible credit what write into book.
Specially these days when
any old crook with a laptop can
cook up a tome. How you
don't pry out that little
pearl in the tusk of a tower where them
letting you earn a dry bread?

Reach for the Scotch with a twist of your wrist
tilt out its poison and sip.

If you don't believe me, you could ask Lady B.

Where is your voice rearranging the air?
Where is Pa's pen putting history down?
Where is the Chief who said to Princess Margaret:
How is you sister these days?

Things just the same: we still have the same
head and same hand with percussion to
lead our parade though the Chief and his
cousin the counsel long gone.

Listen, the government too damn deaf-ears.
Greedy and selfish and too damn deaf-ears.
Black people starving, man. Bakra must
know though him skin colour change
we won't take the licks so.

Searching for Home

In back of my grandparents' house just round
from Tower Street Prison, a fig tree.
Papa and Uncle Lan work in the lock-up.
Them bring home prison bread. It sweet you see!

A holly bush stand to each side
of brick stairs in the fraying front yard.
Dark green elfin leaves sport berries
red like on any Christmas card.

Was a big woman
before it come to me
holly bush have no business
growing in sun-hot—neither it, nor fig tree.

"What leave of British over-lordship,"
say Uncle Norm—Anglican, socialist,
Garveyite, gardening teller of tales
with two teeth. Drink like a fish.
Plant a stone make it grow a stone tree.

"Not so fast," from Aunt V. "Fig tree come
with your Jewish great-great-great-grandma on the run
from murdering Catholics
way cross Atlantic Ocean."

"On the run with a tree?" That is me—
forever too clever for my own good.
"Foolish child!" laugh Aunt V. "It come in her belly!"
She flee breeding a bush? Poor me. Still I don't see.

"Jew there and Jew here is two
different thing." Uncle Norm sigh.
"Where them run from, that hook nose
did mean dread—even dead. Not in this colony.

"Jew here white. And we know white is right
whilst black wretched like sin." (His face
don't agree with his mouth.) "What bout brown?"
I ask, worried. "Brown scrape a parlous place,"

Norm say. "When slavery time done,
bakra anxious for backs to cut cane
so them send to the east. With dot on them
forehead, flowing robes, who arrive but heathen

"with nought but two hand and some
many-armed gods. Black hate them.
White hate them." Uncle Norm
shake him head for him ma was Indian.

Papa say, "So life stay. Pecking order persist,
if not by pigment or purse by some other will.
In prison, common criminal shun intruder.
'Housebreaker? No sir—housebreaker will kill.'"

Canoes come morning time to take
prisoner gangs to Rockfort. Cool breeze,
bright sun, blue sky. Centuries
after we cross that long water, we not free.

One time long time ago slaves sleep
in the deep cellar under this old house—
so them say. Iron rings moored
in stone squint at drifts of grey dust.

Detritus. Duppy lost like Papa,
Uncle Lan, Auntie V, Uncle Norm,
we-self in Canuck cold,
searching for home.

A Poem Is a Power

for Rethabile Masilo

A poem is a power. Invoke it and run the devil. Watch it good . . .
See traces of the first word on it still. Numinous, it will eclipse the
moon, call up mists, halt the sun in high heaven. Listen . . . Hear it
tell sounds we make with our mouth when we propose, with our
hip when we dispose. So use a poem loud for laughter, as a sigh after
ecstasy, time and again for praise. Set it like balm between you and
bad mind with your neighbour. Cause it to gather all who take a knee
for justice, all who genuflect in prayer, all who bow to murder. Blood
bled to born, bloodshed to die. All this in a poem is not too great a
weight.

Poem, Polemic

all like me not writing back to nobody. Pa say anybody, no mind who, address you with less than respect, you not to privilege with neither attention nor reply. same like I not speaking for those who have no voice. is not suppose we suppose to be telling story from God make Adam happy give him Eve for company? as for centre and periphery, them two depend on stage, time, age, if plague still passing or done pass, if fence make to deter a next stray dog or restrain rabblement, barbarian come to breach what armour never reach. look see how much man dead at Benghazi, one so-so white woman but who to know down the road a whole country? you think God easy? is not voice people lack. is ears to hear. absent who dispose to listen, what use to talk back, talk for all who can't talk, talk from anywhere to anywhere?

Poem Ascending

Poets make up things tell tales pass history. Is mystery they reckon.
It have no way to find the tell-tale truth but slash green skin chop
coir through crack nut and suck trembling white flesh. What a thing,
eh? That young sweet shivering—no not in truth it neither sweet nor
salt nor have no taste to chronicle. Instead a blessing of the tongue
and then slide round and round the mouth and down the throat and
down down down . . . till the root shoot—

poem ascending.

Stalking Ma

1
My mother was a walker. When she
take to the road, one of us follow her.
Somebody in the house call Pa.

No grown-up ever follow Ma—
just one of us. And never once the boys.
"Is you to go this time. Last time was me."

"No sir! Not such a thing. Remember
she see me last time, we fuss, and little most
she shove me down in front the bus?"

Suck teeth. Cut eye. Socks and school shoes
(our Sunday shoes the other pair)
and out the gate and far enough behind

so Ma don't catch no glimpse of me.
Until—until she and me see Pa car.
Ma always see and never see us stalk her.

2
I never thought what Mama thought
climbing past yellow sidewalk stones
of tribulation buttercups aka fever plant

and puncture vine. How sun hot never
stop her neither shame nor neighbours
laughing at her pouch of dear belongings

tied into a square of bright red cloth
stuck on a stick just like the picture
of Dick Whittington in our story book.

3
Ma knew the whole road knew.
She never cared. Her bag hoisted upon its pole,
she made her journey all the same.

We gave her wide berth toiling in sunhot
up, up longside that everlasting hill,
dodging inside a gateway,

round a tree, stooped to inhale
a garbage can if she turned
back to look.

4
She never got away. Pa's boasie Buick
inventoried us just in time, rescued
our pride, nosing us home to wait

for Dr Cope to come with magic pills and papers
for asylum. Ma went again and went again.
Whatever drove her never went.

5
When she was well she worked.
Never worked long, this work
—a couple weeks, a month.

Then she was home. She ran
her household never mind. Wrote
clothes into the laundry book. Checked for

fifteen dark pairs of socks, nine light,
ten undershirts, a dozen handkerchiefs. Made meals
of just enough for six, then seven of us, then eight.

6

And Ma grew gladioli a mutiny
of orange, pink, mauve, yellow,
purple, rebel blooms

stuck their tongues out
at Pa, the neighbours,
Dr Cope and us.

7

I never knew Ma hated sex or so Pa said
or made believe for make belief enables transports,
trammels up the dreadful ordinary of our lives.

Pa got it somewhere else.
Respectable. A decent light skin girl
in the church choir. Clean house. Clean life.

Pussy preserved for Pa in hope his wife
might die, God forbid, by her very hand
or mercifully by the Lord's decree.

Well harsh is true but nothing new
one woman wish a next one ill
so she can have her way.

Is so it stay since time begin
and Mother Eve make Adam sin
and God take sex and make revenge.

8

Is only right any woman
who take away a next one man
get curse up every street,

cross each backyard, down each last
lane, and if it come to that, and out of sight
of Babylon, licks in her skin.

But how exact revenge upon a faceless wretch?
Why Ma should share Pa with a stranger
she could not abuse? Fair after all is fair.

9
Ma wasn't fair. She was a dark brown girl,
her head of hair thicked black with curls,
her blood a puddled mud not of her making.

10
I step and step and step up the dry road,
my blistering feet a fire, my head a rock,
my eight year old heart breaking.

Walk a Short Way wid Dis Sistren:
A Conversation with the Editors

STEPHANIE MCKENZIE: I just want to begin by saying, Carol, that this conversation with you seems so in keeping with Pamela Mordecai's work. It seems to me that Mordecai has been having a conversation with her public, perhaps in particular with women, for her entire career now. It's her spoken word, her capturing of spoken exchange, that has often grabbed my attention the most.

CAROL BAILEY: Yes indeed, Stephanie; the interplay between orature and literature has been a defining element of Mordecai's work. In the introductory essay of *Her True-True Name*,[*] Mordecai and Betty Wilson note that one of the contributions women writers have made to the Caribbean literary tradition is the way in which they have used informal artistic modes, thus foregrounding vernacular forms as literary aesthetic. Mordecai has really been part of that generation of writers. She has set in motion and helped to establish a locally inspired Creole ground on which other writers can build, and that's why it's so significant that Tanya Shirley has contributed an afterword for this book—having a younger voice as the closing act, so to speak, illustrates the arc of Caribbean women's writing. This attentiveness to vernacular traditions is part of what makes Mordecai such a significant figure in Caribbean literature.

SM: I'm reminded here of an anecdote which Mordecai shared with us. As a young woman she met Louise Bennett when Mordecai was walking into the Jamaica Broadcasting Service studio to record programs for the Jamaica Information Service when Miss Lou was walking out, having recorded episodes for "Ring Ding," her famous Jamaican children's program. For me, that metaphorically captures a glimpse into the passing on of a baton, or the possibility of doing so. And of

---

[*] *Her True-True Name: An Anthology of Women's Writing from the Caribbean*, edited by Pamela Mordecai and Betty Wilson, Heinemann, 1989.

course, the influence of Bennett on Mordecai's poetry is now indisputable. I'm reminded, too, of the story Mordecai shared with us when talking about her poetic inspirations even as a child. She'd memorize and recite Bennett's poems, her father joking and saying that, because they were in Jamaica Patwa, they would get her nowhere. This recalls the story Mervyn Morris recounts about Miss Lou: "At one of her early performances a voice called out, 'A dat yuh modder sen yuh a school fah?'"* There is a lot of Bennett in Mordecai's poetry, perhaps, most importantly, a refusal to give up a particular, innovative voice in the interests of serving some outside "standard."

CB: Can I ask if there was a particular poem or aspect of her work that compelled you to pursue this project?

SM: As a feminist, I was drawn to her subject matter and her dedication to women's rights and human rights. Her oeuvre also includes so many types of metrics, so many subjects. The range of technical forms between *Journey Poem* and *The True Blue of Islands* and *Certifiable* is so impressive. Mordecai, to me, is a technician of the form who follows no guiding principle. Unpredictability is the predictable. Just when you think to yourself, "Okay, this is the kind of poet she is," poof! She has started an entirely different kind of collection. And then of course there's the honesty and the emotion at her core and— Tanya speaks about this, too—an irreverence, but coupled with such a love of human nature and human beings. I am so bowled over, too, by her boundless vocabulary. I don't know if anyone's written about it yet, but this is another thing that really strikes me about her poems.

CB: I, too, am struck by her vocabulary, and I think one of the things that I keep hearing when I read her poetry, being particularly attentive to her vocabulary, is the colonial education system being put to its best use. Mordecai is among the islanders who received a very deep and rigorous grammar-school education through the colonial system but, notably, emerged

---

* See Mervyn Morris, "Miss Lou and Why She Matters" on the National Library of Jamaica website (https://nlj.gov.jm).

as a critic of the system, rather than an apologist for it. But in terms of having a wide vocabulary, in terms of connecting with language—she brings that formal education and her rooted-ness as a Jamaican, a culturally grounded Jamaican, together quite constructively with subversive explosiveness.

SM: Yes, that's a very important point—that she received a signif-icant "mix" of schooling. I'm thinking of a substantial email she sent to us, and I think it's important to quote her at length here: "I went to Alpha Academy, one of Kingston's three down-town high schools at the time—very different from Kings-ton's uptown schools. I would not be who I am if I had gone to Immaculate or St. Andrew or St. Hugh's. Alpha was one of the first places in the island to create indigenous theatre in the late nineteenth century. It had a strong emphasis on the arts. I did a lot of acting and reciting because the school took part in the annual All Island Speech Festival and the Schools Drama Festival. Plus, Alpha was part of a vast complex of many different schools that represented a cross section of Jamaican society, including 'industrial' schools for boys and girls, some of whom were wards of the court. Many of Jamaica's musicians who emerged in the last half to three quarter century went to Alpha Boys School. Singers, too, like Yellow Man" (email cor-respondence, November 5, 2021).* Of course, Mordecai would later go to Newton College of the Sacred Heart in 1960, at the start of the Civil Rights Movement. As she explained to us, too, she "went on scholarship, one of seven or eight women who integrated a prestigious Catholic College run by the Mes-dames du Sacré Coeur—an order founded in France to teach the daughters of the rich. . . . The Kennedy women went to colleges run by these nuns." And though she was "profoundly unhappy," she received an excellent education. These experi-ences are so different than those I had being raised in Canada, Carol. I've lived in Jamaica for different periods of time, but I wasn't raised there. And there are certain experiences, when you're not raised in a culture, that you're not going to fully

---

* See also Pamela Mordecai, "Falling in Love with Poetry" in *The New Quarterly*, Issue 156, Fall 2020.

understand. I noticed that, when we were comparing poem choices over the years, you would cleave to certain poems, perhaps, one could say, those most rooted in a Jamaican sensibility. I learned a lot about having to question myself about my own aesthetics and how aesthetics are often culturally shaped. Would you say that a shared Jamaican heritage with Mordecai led to certain poems resonating with you more than others?

CB: Mordecai's rootedness in Jamaican speech culture, and the culture in general, is a point of connection for me. There are two things I'd like to pick up on: What it means to be inside an aesthetic culture and how you hear and appreciate works, but also what you learn from someone who hears those cultural associations and resonances but hears them in a different way. And you brought an air of the insider/outsider because you've lived in Jamaica and you've heard people talk on the streets and you've heard different cadences, rhythms, and expressive modes. The thing that was most helpful for me working with you was getting the perspective of an actual creative writer who thinks about the work in a different way, being the poet, the facilitator, and the critic. I was more like a cultural insider, but you were like a genre insider.

And to your question about a shared heritage, these cultural resonances and the rootedness in orature are, in part, what I find so compelling about the poems in *de Man, de book of Mary,* and *de book of Joseph*: Just the titles of those poems are so subversive—speaking of *Subversive Sonnets*—and so representative of what I said earlier about Mordecai bringing her colonial education, her British education, and her commitment to her Caribbean vernacular culture together. Writing the poems in Creole and taking on biblical stories—Mordecai's engagement with sacred subjects is well known—and infusing them with the history and sociocultural themes of the Caribbean all shapes the power of her art. I found those three collections captivating, rooted, and resonant, in terms of how the poems are grounded in the spiritual culture of the Jamaican community; how the poems engage with the colonial part of ourselves; and how Mordecai is able to weave all of these things together into what I consider to be one of the best possible ways to do creative writing. I would highlight those poems—where the Creole voice is most pronounced—as some of the ones that I find most compelling stylistically.

SM: *de Man* is such a powerful work. Why don't we talk about *de Man* and the challenges that were involved in making selections. I can remember that we made and remade those selections a number of times.

CB: Yes, I do, too. It was a good problem for us to have because there were so many strong pieces. We really wanted the selections to represent the collection as best as possible, and to demonstrate Mordecai's poetic range. I think the part of choosing that was the most challenging was considering this *range* in different ways: a range of voices, range of subject matter, range of perspectives. But I think what helped us navigate that knotty part of the selection process was our shared admiration for how Pamela foregrounds women. That is, for both of us, a central part of Pamela's disruptive irreverence.

SM: There's also the wonderful subplot in *de Man*: Samuel who's lovesick for Naomi, who still thinks fondly of Samuel; Samuel who suffers from physical challenges, with a chopped-off hand. Pontius Pilate's wife is a strong figure, and then there's Naomi herself, of course, who's a really well-rounded character. It was important to include those stories, as it's really in the subplots that readers are made aware that women are no shrinking violets. Behind her husband's back, Pilate's wife has ordered Naomi to report to her. He's described as a "frog- / face," and she's one that has "de commonsense" ("Station I: Jesus Is Condemned to Death"). Then, there's *de book of Joseph*. Despite the title, it's again the women I connect to the most and in the little subplots where I smile and pay most attention. One of my favorite scenes in that book is when Debs, Joseph's first wife, after having seen so many of her babies die, wants to make more babies with Joseph. The poem seems mournful at first but, by the end of the poem, the focus shifts to her physical passions. After Joseph expresses concern that he doesn't want her to be pregnant again (for fear of losing another child and of the possible harm to his wife's body), "Debs push [Joseph] down flat." I laughed aloud. This woman is guided by both desire and her skill in shaping decisions.

CB: I laughed out loud after reading that line too, and found myself reading it over and over. *de book of Joseph* is yet another masterpiece from Mordecai. It won't surprise you, Stephanie, that I'm captivated by her deft use of language in this work—the way Jamaican Creole defamiliarizes the conventions of the biblical story to draw readers into the imagined narrative. I, too, am struck by the way gender is treated in this work: Mordecai takes a Womanist approach. As you note, women's leadership is skillfully highlighted while, at the same time, we experience Joseph as a thoughtful human being—a man intimately connected to his feelings and to the wellbeing of his wives.

SM: Yes, I also feel one of Mordecai's greatest talents is how her poetry encourages readers to defamiliarize, to see ordinary things in a new way and canonical stories in a new light. This trait seems in keeping, too, with Mordecai's academic output, most notably her PhD dissertation, *Prismatic Vision: Aspects of Imagery, Language and Structure in the Poetry of Kamau Brathwaite and Derek Walcott* (1977), where she coined the term "prismatic vision" to speak of "a Caribbean style of cognition." It is that ability to see through new prisms, to translate into a new way of understanding sacred stories that makes Mordecai's poetry stand out.

CB: Yes, that skill brilliantly shines through in both *de book of Joseph*, which weaves together so many tales, and in *de Man*, in which we see a mother wrestling with losing her child. Mordecai transforms these traditional biblical chronicles into vivid, relatable family stories.

SM: Absolutely. In *de Man*, for example, the focus is really on Mary—the tortuous emotional drama of a mother who is losing her son. That stands out more than—and I don't mean this to sound blasphemous—the crucifixion itself. I also want to mention something else here: Mordecai's precocious intellect. She wrote *de Man* almost two decades before the New Testament was translated into Jamaican Creole.* Now, I'd like to ask you a tough question: Do you have a favorite poem in *A Fierce Green Place*?

CB: Oh my goodness. Maybe it would be one of the family-themed poems. There's one, "Temitope," that she wrote to her daughter when her daughter was expecting a daughter. I have so many favorites—there's another poem about the University of the West Indies.

SM: "Chinese Gardens—UWI"?

CB: Yes, that one certainly strikes a deep chord in me. You see I'm struggling because I have no one favorite, but that one's surely up there.

SM: Her line, "I come feet naked to the sun"—if I could write one line like that in my career, I'd be happy.

CB: It's like the title of Michelle Cliff's lyrical essay "If I Could Write This in Fire, I Would Write This in Fire." It's one of those lines, those career-making lines. It's like when Toni Morrison uses the word "rememory,"** it's that kind of thing. It's that kind of genre-making, memorable line.

SM: I'm just hoping this *New and Selected* will draw wider attention to her work—it will surely have a lasting impact in world literature. With the two most celebrated Caribbean poets Kamau Brathwaite and Derek Walcott gone now, where do you see Mordecai's poetry in this tradition? Of course, there is the great and internationally acclaimed poet Lorna Goodison, too, as well as a number of well-canonized authors, such as Olive Senior and Grace Nichols, and there is a vibrant coterie of emerging writers, but . . . Mordecai has been writing for years and her work has not circulated as widely as the work of others for several reasons. She's been published exclusively by small

---

* *Di Jamiekan Nyuu Testiment*, The Bible Society of the West Indies, 2012.
** Toni Morrison, *Beloved*, Knopf, 1987.

presses. She moved with her family to Canada in 1994 and exists more or less in the margins of the literary scene there. She hasn't been part of the conference circuit, no doubt related to the fact that she hasn't been consistently part of the academic world where writer-professors, for example, have access to university funding for their books, travel, and launches, and where they can easily foster connections that allow for consistent access to reading invitations. She's devoted time to promoting the work of others as an anthologist and a small-press publisher, and, of course, there is the world she was born into—where women's voices, particularly from the Caribbean, haven't been as readily embraced. This is the first time a good representation of her poetry will circulate internationally, outside of Canada and the Caribbean. To return to my question: Where do you situate Mordecai's work in the history of Caribbean literature?

CB: I would place her right at the top among all of the major writers. Generationally, I would definitely see Mordecai as one of the trailblazers, in terms of form and subject matter. Her boldness is palpable. It was actually while working on *A Fierce Green Place* that I truly appreciated her irreverence. I heard Tanya Shirley read and I realized that the subject matter that Shirley takes on—how she writes about women in the dance-hall in a liberatory way, how she writes a very tender poem about a mother with her gay son, how she writes about sexuality and immigration, and how she brings all those things together—has its precursor in someone like Mordecai, who has paved the way for that kind of writing in women's literature. So I see her definitely as foundational. I see her, in terms of craft, as exemplary, and as an astute thinker. And Mordecai brings this astute mind to her poetry; she brings her vast vocabulary. I see her as part of the apex of Caribbean literature and definitely the apex of Caribbean women's writing. I think all of us, whether we come at this literature from criticism or we come at it as creative writers, we owe Mordecai an enormous debt of gratitude because she has given us so much on which to build.

[This conversation was recorded in December 2020. It was subsequently transcribed, added to, and edited for clarity and flow. The editors would like to thank Teri-Ann McDonald for making the transcription that gave our words legs, and for her job over the years as an incomparable copy editor, including her valuable work on this edition as a whole.]

Afterword

At her reading from *Subversive Sonnets* at Kingston's Bookland in 2014, Pamela Mordecai was asked by an audience member to justify her use of profanity based on her Catholic education. Mordecai's response was that she's always considered herself to be a rebel. This selection of poems across her writing life reveals Mordecai's interest in many of the dominant thematic concerns of Caribbean literature; however, it may be argued that her treatment of rebellious poetics sets her aside from many of her female counterparts. In "Pamela Mordecai's Poetry: Some Questions for Further Consideration," Stephanie McKenzie notes that there is a "lacuna in the criticism of Mordecai's work." I must admit that it was not until I began pursuing graduate studies in literature that I encountered Mordecai, and even then, it was in her role as an anthologist. It is only recently that scholars have begun to give her poetry the critical attention it deserves.

The Caribbean female poets who emerged alongside Mordecai in the 1980s had the difficult task of inserting themselves into a Caribbean literary tradition primarily defined by patriarchal representations of postcolonialism, which manifested themselves in a preoccupation with nationalism and male-identity politics. These female poets sought to address the omissions and expand the scope of those dominant narratives. Poets like Dionne Brand, Jean "Binta" Breeze, Lorna Goodison, Grace Nichols, Olive Senior, and their forerunner Louise Bennett repositioned the role and concerns of women in the discourse. Although Pamela Mordecai's first poetry collection, *Journey Poem*, was published in 1989, her name is seldom mentioned in the preceding list of canonical Anglo-Caribbean female poets. The works of these poets continue to be examined contextually in terms of the rebellious nature of their personae, whether they're against a heteronormative brand of sexuality, the systemic oppression of slavery, the inequitable hierarchy of female labour, or the lack of attention given to issues that affect women. They are also discussed in terms of the rebellious nature of their poetic style. The female poets of the 1980s experimented with tropes, forms, and language in order to create poetry that would more accurately portray their reality and perspectives. I wonder, however, if Mordecai's work was too rebellious.

As critics of Caribbean literature, even as we privilege the treatment of African cosmology, are we still marginalizing the work of female poets whose form of rebellion may be too far outside European norms of propriety? In Mordecai's exploration of violence, particularly the neocolonial sexual trauma inflicted upon Black women by Black men, is there a heaviness that, as Caribbean people, we are not yet ready to confront? Does the female sensibility of Mordecai's work dangle too precariously outside the margins of acceptable social norms?

I do not have the answers as to why Mordecai has not received the critical attention her work deserves, but I do know that it is not because her work lacks the technical adroitness or the thorough investment in topics relevant to the study of Caribbean literature. For example, the poems included here from Mordecai's very first collection, *Journey Poem,* introduce a poet who is invested in portraying the intersectionality between personal and public histories and who, in doing so, expresses a vulnerability indicative of the postcolonial psyche. This vulnerability is apparent in "Walker" and "Family Story," in which the persona expounds on the theme of mental illness that runs in her family, but instead of the apologetic tone that often accompanies these confessions, she uses her father's resilience and her mother's "whimsy" as fodder to construct a fearless self: "Careful then / how you cross me." The use of a menacing tone is a recurring stylistic device in Mordecai's work. The early poems provide the foundation that justifies the representation of woman as the prophetic voice of damnation if there is no penance or restitution.

The trope of the fearless woman is also accentuated early in Mordecai's career, as in *Journey Poem*'s "Island Woman" and "Poem." Mordecai portrays the complexity of living in a "fierce green place" through the persona's metaphorical embodiment of the landscape. Regardless of internal and external turmoil, "each year after the rains / I blossom." This woman is also an embodiment of poetry, and—although I am reluctant to read poetry by women in a way that positions their work as always responding to writing by men—it is obvious that "Poem" is in dialogue with Edward Kamau Brathwaite's poems and theories regarding African retention in Caribbean literature. Mordecai's poem, like Brathwaite's "The Making of the Drum," privileges the symbiotic relationship between the drum and the artist/musician. However,

Mordecai reimagines the spiritual practice of making art as one that emerges from the womb. Though the transatlantic winds symbolize historical trauma, the female has the potential to tap into the womb-space (similar to the gourd in Olive Senior's poems or the kumbla in Erna Brodber's fiction) in order to manifest an interpretation of the creation myth that writes woman into the origins of language, sound, and power. The cyclical process of creating the drum in Brathwaite's poem is aligned in Mordecai's poems with the female reproductive cycle.

Mordecai's poems illustrate the heavy responsibility of writing out of this womb-space. Even in the elegiac poems in *The True Blue of Islands*, it is the woman who must reconcile her religious indoctrination with her brother's senseless murder and a people who "grit [their] teeth / and carry on through" ("Everybody Get Flat—A Dub"). In her interrogation of the theme of violence in all her collections, Mordecai employs explicit imagery, the performative and guttural resonances of dub, the improvisation of jazz and blues, and the subversion of traditional poetic forms, such as the sonnet, to create an uncomfortable representation of "female sensibility." Mordecai deserves recognition for perforating the boundaries of Caribbean female poetry to allow the inclusion of the profane and thereby forcing readers to re-examine their stereotypical notions of acceptable female articulation. The graphic image of sexual violence meted out to the persona in "Convent Girl" and other poems is an indictment of societal norms that continue to encourage the subjugation of women. Mordecai's use of profanity, dialect, Rastafarian idioms, and harsh alliteration work together to subvert notions of acceptable female poetic expression.

Perhaps what is most surprising about Mordecai's work, considering her religious upbringing and the psychosocial acceptance of religious belief in the Caribbean, is her interrogation of religious doctrine and willingness to rewrite Christian narratives from a Caribbean perspective; *de Man, de book of Mary,* and *de book of Joseph* function as a demystification of the birth, crucifixion, and resurrection of Jesus. In Caribbean societies, where the role of nation languages is still being debated, Mordecai's performance poems in Jamaican Creole may be read as a radical act of communal self-acceptance and a privileging of the ordinary folk who have been disenfranchised in the history of the

Caribbean. The poems make room for the personae and audiences to question entrenched biblical narratives and ironically, if they choose to do so, strengthen their faith through the act of seeing themselves reflected in the scenes. Mordecai's theoretical work expounds on the function of plurality in Caribbean literature and it is one of her greatest achievements in her poetry: the ability to pile on images, to portray the paradoxes of human existence, to create stanzas that reject reconciliation, to represent the people, culture, and topography of the Caribbean in multidimensional, complex ways.

—*Tanya Shirley*

Author's Notes

page 85   ***Lace Makers***: Claude McKay, Jamaica's first important twentieth-century poet and novelist, is the first Jamaican writer of significance to use the vernacular in his work. He is well known to Jamaican students, myself among them, for the nostalgic "Flame Heart," to which my poem refers.

88   ***Cockpit Country—A Tasting Tour***: The "eerie and unusual landscape of the Cockpit Country" occurs in the interior of Jamaica. "The cockpits are steep sided valleys that alternate with conical hillocks to form a . . . Karst topography. . . . Streams and rivers flow underground and sinkholes and caves are characteristic of the area." Cockpit Country encompasses roughly 500 square miles (1,300 square kilometres), "and much of it remains unexplored" (Olive Senior, *Encyclopedia of Jamaican Heritage*, 2003, 114–15).

94   ***temitope***: (origin Yoruba) Enough to give thanks; give thanks to God. It is a name for both males and females, though more often females.

95   ***igba***: rope; two hundred; time/season; garden egg.

   Olorun: Creator, Supreme Being, one of the many names for the Yoruba Sky God.

106   ***Thomas Thistlewood and Tom***: Thomas Thistlewood came to Jamaica from Lincolnshire where, according to Susanna O'Neill, the residents are "known by the delightful nickname Yellowbellies" (*Folklore of Lincolnshire*, 2012, 131–32). While the origin of the nickname is debated, O'Neill notes that it may "have originated because the waistcoat of the Lincolnshire Regiment's uniform was yellow."

149   ***de book of Joseph***: I took the idea of Joseph as a widower from apocryphal writings, which also provide the story of how God chooses him as Mary's husband. I imagine Joseph marrying in his late teens, taking a bride chosen for him, to whom, as was customary, he is betrothed for a year before she comes to live in his father's house. Joseph's first wife, Debs/Miss Deborah, and the story of their married life, is entirely my creation. In my account, he becomes a *young* widower when Debs dies. The Gospels of Matthew and Luke are the sources for Mary's betrothal to Joseph, his decision to put her aside when he discovers she is pregnant, and his marriage to her on God's instruction. The poems also broadly follow the gospel accounts of the birth of Jesus, the flight into Egypt and the return. Non-canonical *details* of these events are imagined, with some help from lore, as is the tale of the rest of Joseph's life and his death.

182   ***True-True Love***: Below is the poem that inspired mine.

True Love
by Edward Baugh

You lament that you will never know
what it is to go to sleep with me
beside you, and wake up in the morning
to find me there. Consider, love, you will
have had the best of me, the passion
and the tenderness that you command;
not have my body's frailties to endure:
hear me break wind, and belch, and snore,
and, after all that, have to love me still.

(from *Black Sand: New and Selected Poems*, Peepal Tree Press, 2013)

185   ***Transcribing the letters of William Alexander Bustamante***: Sir William Alexander Bustamante, the flamboyant first prime minister of Jamaica and first Jamaican National Hero, was familiarly known as "Busta" or "Chief." He began his involvement in public life by publishing a series of letters about political and social conditions in colonial Jamaica in *The Daily Gleaner* and *The Jamaica Standard* newspapers. Bustamante had little formal education: as *The Encyclopedia of Jamaican Heritage* indicates, "His education and opportunities were limited" (82). Lady Bustamante confirms in her biography that he had scribes, of which she was one, writing letters that K. O'Brien Chang characterized as displaying "an impressive range of knowledge, an ordered mind and a lively wit" (*The Gleaner*, 31 July 2012). Certainly, it was known in our family that our father, Louis Hitchins, was a ghost writer for Busta, though, as far as I am aware, this is not documented in any accounts of Bustamante's life. They met in the downtown surgery of a dentist friend, Dr. Evans, where Bustamante dictated the letters and my father edited and transcribed them.

Marie Ponsot: The American poet and translator Marie Ponsot was born in Queens, New York, in 1921 and died in 2019. When I heard her read fifteen or twenty years ago, she did not strike me as a woman of her years. I was struck by a poem in dactyls she shared at the NYC reading. Dactyls are demanding. Commenting on her use of form, she said in a 1999 *New York Times* interview, "The forms . . . are not restrictive. They pull things out of you. They help you remember." Those feelings are pretty close to my own.

Index of Titles and First Lines

(Titles are in italic)

Acknowledgements

I am grateful to my late husband, Martin, who has helped me to re-
fine almost everything I have ever written; to my daughter, Rachel,
who, apart from Martin, has been my most consistent critic, and my
sisters, Betty and Mary, who have been faithful reviewers, on and off,
throughout my writing life; to my sons, David and Daniel, for their
indulgence of a writer-mother; and to the taxpayers of Toronto, On-
tario, and Canada, through the Toronto Arts Council, the Ontario Arts
Council, and the Canada Council, for their steady funding of my writ-
ing over decades. Thanks, too, to Grenfell Campus, Memorial Univer-
sity of Newfoundland, for providing funding during the latter stages
of preparation of this manuscript. Space does not permit me to say
thanks to the many people who made the original collections possi-
ble (all of these publications listed elsewhere in this book) or to the
friends, colleagues, and well-wishers who have encouraged my efforts
by commenting on, promoting, and on occasion translating the po-
ems over many years. They know who they are and I hope they know
I am deeply grateful. I am indebted to the late Kamau Brathwaite,
George Elliott Clarke, Carol Duncan, Lissa Paul, Seanna Sumalee
Oakley, Elaine Savory, Olive Senior, and Tim Reiss for their ongoing
support as beta readers and/or teachers and/or critics of the poems.
I am delighted that Tanya Shirley so generously consented to pro-
vide the perspective of a woman poet of a younger generation in her
afterword. I thank Edward Baugh and Peepal Tree Press for permis-
sion to use "True Love" from his *Black Sand: New and Selected Poems.*
JonArno Lawson, the ON-7 poetry-writing group, Pat Penn Hilden,
Betty Wilson, and in particular, Edward Baugh, Rachel Mordecai, and
Sarah Tolmie cast keen eyes on various poems in *A Fierce Green Place.*
I am in their debt. Finally, I especially thank Stephanie McKenzie for
teaching, writing about, and promoting my work in so many ways,
and for suggesting this project, Carol Bailey for coming on board as
coeditor, and Teri-Ann McDonald for navigating the craft, once it set
sail, and keeping the crew on task. Tim Reiss steadfastly kept the light
on in the lighthouse. That the manuscript found safe harbour at New

Directions is providential; our pilot, Jeffrey Yang, steered it expertly into dock. Any listing or leaking is, as always, up to me. May God bless us all and keep us safe in capricious waters!

Pamela Mordecai has published seven collections of poetry, five children's books, and a collection of short fiction, *Pink Icing*, first published by Insomniac Press and recently released as an audiobook read by herself in ECW Press's Bespeak Audio Editions. Her eighth collection, *de book of Joseph: a performance poem*, is forthcoming from Mawenzi House (Toronto) in June 2022. Her debut novel, *Red Jacket*, was shortlisted for the Rogers Writers' Trust Fiction Award, one of Canada's top prizes for literary fiction. Mordecai is well known internationally for her children's poems, which have been widely anthologized as well as used in language-arts curricula in the Caribbean, India, Malaysia, the UK, the USA, and South and West Africa. A veteran anthologist with several collections to her credit, she has a special interest in the writing of Caribbean women. She has published numerous language-arts textbooks for the Caribbean, most of them with the late Grace Walker-Gordon. A play for children, *El Numero Uno or the Pig from Lopinot,* had its world premiere at the Young People's Theatre in Toronto in 2010 and its Caribbean premiere at the Edna Manley School for the Performing Arts in Kingston in 2016. With her late husband Martin, Mordecai wrote *Culture and Customs of Jamaica* in a series edited by Peter Standish, originally for Greenwood Press. A trained language-arts teacher with a PhD in English, she was for many years publications officer in the Faculty of Education, the University of the West Indies, and publications editor of the *Caribbean Journal of Education*. She has also worked in media, especially television. In 2015, Mordecai was filmed reading her first five poetry collections, as well as some poems and stories for children. The videorecordings can be accessed at https://mordecai.citl.mun.ca. She lives in Toronto and has three children and a granddaughter.

Carol Bailey is an associate professor in the English Department at Westfield State University in Massachusetts, where she teaches courses in World, Postcolonial, Caribbean and Cross-Cultural, and Women's Literatures. She is the author of *A Poetics of Performance: The Oral-Scribal Aesthetic in Anglophone Caribbean Fiction* (UWI Press, 2014) and *Writing the Black Diasporic City in the Age of Globalization* (Rutgers, forthcoming).

Stephanie McKenzie is the author of three books of poetry (all published by Salmon Poetry) and a literary monograph, *Before the Country: Native Renaissance, Canadian Mythology* (University of Toronto Press, 2007; Rpt. 2019). She is a professor in the English Programme at Grenfell Campus, Memorial University of Newfoundland.

Tanya Shirley has published two poetry collections with Peepal Tree Press in the UK: *She Who Sleeps With Bones* and *The Merchant of Feathers*. Her work has been featured on BBC World Service and The Poetry Archive, and has been translated into Spanish and Polish. She has conducted writing workshops and performed in the UK, Canada, the Caribbean, Venezuela, and the USA. She lectures at the University of the West Indies, Mona Campus, and is a proud Cave Canem fellow.

Teri-Ann McDonald is a copy and substantive editor who has worked on numerous monographs, anthologies, and journal articles. She was a production editor for *Descant*, Canada's bestselling literary anthology. McDonald has also worked with Royal Society of Canada members and Order of Canada Companions to produce works published by Oxford UP, Columbia UP, and Peter Lang, among others.